From Grief to Grace

Overcoming The Pain of Trauma, Loss & Transition

By Evelyn Rai

Published in the United States by In Writing Publications, LLC

https://inwritingpublicationsllc.com

nwritingpublications@gmail.com

ISBN: 978-0-578-30176-1 (Paperback)
Copyright © September 2021

Library of Congress Control Number: 2021920232

Cover Credit: Girt Enterprises, LLC
No copyright infringement intended.

Foreword

By Dr. Eric Yancy

It has been my pleasure to know Evelyn Rai for nearly four decades. As a pediatrician early in my practice, she entrusted to me the most valuable asset any parent could have; the health of her child. A devoted mother in every way, I still remember some of our encounters in my office as she sought the most effective care for her children.

In this account, From Grief to Grace, Evelyn takes us on an incredible journey. The saying "into each life some rain must fall" was brought to vivid reality at the death of her son, Joshua. The monsoons of pain soaking every inch of her being could have broken her spirit. Indeed, it left her standing in puddles of despair and bitterness pooling around her feet.

Instead of focusing on the "mud" she instead chose to focus on the "mission". In this volume she speaks in great detail of how she allowed the Light of "The Sun" to transform the mud of hopelessness into the bricks' determination. She provides a step-by-step guide of how to go from the depths of grief to realize and embrace one's passion and one's mission.

Evelyn masterfully outlines the tortuous path of elevation from unspeakable grief to unshakable faith. Certainly, this book will resonate with those who have experienced loss in the past. But it will also provide a certain amount of pre-emptive preparation, as at some point we will all experience circumstances that cause us pain.

It was a pleasure to have been a part of her beloved son, Joshua's life. And it remains my pleasure to know such a wonderful, insightful, servant of The Most High God. While you may identify with her tears, you will also celebrate her triumph.

Enjoy "From Grief To Grace". I certainly did.

Dedication

This book is dedicated to the memory and honor of my firstborn son, Joshua Lee Cosby, and to my grandchildren whom he loves, Caleb Lee, Ella Jolei, Caleb Adams, and Breanna Lanae. To his brother and only sibling, Daylen Joel, whom Joshua dearly loved, protected as a guardian angel and enjoyed being his big brother. To his cousin, Taiyon Dodson, who was raised like a sister and his chief confidant. To the father of my sons, Isadore Lee, and former husband, who demonstrated his love and care by supporting our little family. To the many friends, co-workers, and relatives that have been touched by Joshua's life and spirit.

To Mothers and Fathers everywhere who have experienced "*soul trauma*" due to the death of a child(ren), sudden or unexpected. Above all this book is dedicated to my Creator, The I Am, (Adonai/El Shaddai) The Father/Mother of all Souls, for His/Her unfailing eternal Love and for allowing me these privileges of the human experiences. There are no words to convey the depth of my gratitude to You for giving me the Divine Breath of Light, Love, and Understanding on this journey called "L.I.F.E." Living In Faith Everyday!

All Praises to our Creator, The All, The Most High Elohim!

Contents

Preface

To everything, there is a season, and a time to every purpose under heaven: A time to be born, and a time to die.

— Ecclesiastes 3:1.

My Why

This is my candid, but transparent sharing of myself with you my reader. I've always been a "different kinda duck", Lol! Over the course of my life, I have learned to embrace that reality. Today we have language and terminology that aptly describes my world growing up. Words like "empath" whereas when I was a child, I was called an "Old Soul" because I was always sitting around the adults and speaking with them like I was one. I could invariably be found either tending to the babies "nurturing" them, or assisting the elders. We now say things like "intuitive" or "intuition", but as a child, we'd say it's a "sixth sense", or "something told me" and "I got that feeling". When a dream turns into a life experience, we'd say it's "Deja Vu". In religion, when a person would tell a matter, as matter of fact, before it happened, we'd say he's/she's a "seer" or they have the "gift", they're a "prophet or prophetess". Grandma or Auntie dreaming about fishes definitely meant someone was pregnant. Culturally, these things were normal for me as a child and I now know for many others. We had a sense beyond our physical senses that made us connect in ways that at times were unexplainable.

So on the morning of Joshua's "Celebration of Life" service, (his funeral service), while in the shower sobbing uncontrollably, numbed by the searing pain of soul-trauma, dismay, bitterness and grief, I screamed out to *Father*, "I don't understand!!! Why didn't you tell me?! You always tell me things! Things about people and their lives, and I don't even ask to know. You know I know Your ways with me! WHY???!!! Weeping with a pain so deep, the next breath seemed almost non existent. You know like a small child that has just had a total meltdown and can only huff their breaths with the body's full assistance, that was my state. Then I heard within my being so gently that familiar voice... "I did tell you."

I was incensed! When, when did you tell me? I searched my mind like a wild person trying to find the light of this truth (the mind is so powerful!) I couldn't gather one moment of understanding until... I remembered *the dream*.

Left to right: Joshua Lee, Evelyn Rai, Daylen Joel

Introduction

The purpose of this writing is to encourage the reader to know that the pain of grief, as real as it is, has a divine purpose for the human soul. That there is a process to grieving and there are healthy and unhealthy ways to have the experience.

In sharing my personal account, I hope to inspire an approach that allows for the embracing of the soul's pain to give life and provide new insight and fresh understanding to the power of the Human Spirit which never dies. To reveal the deeper meanings of *"...Though he were dead, yet shall he live;"* and *"whosoever believes in me shall never die."*

This book will empower the reader to courageously examine themselves and the circumstances which brought them to this book. It will cause the reader to question whether or not their current philosophy of life is adequately serving them in the process of their grief experience. If not, what's the alternative? The reader will be challenged in their definitions of *"Death"*, *"Loss"*, and *"Transition"* and how these terms can directly affect their process.

Finally, I will warn the reader that some parts of this book may not resonate depending on their stage within the grief process and their spiritual acuity. Because grief is a trauma to the soul (psyche), where the seat of our emotions live, and the nature of death is both spiritual and physical, it demands a reckoning with one's belief system. I will provoke thought as to what is *"Believed"* about death versus what is *"Known"* about death. I will ask the reader to be mindful (to think about what they're thinking about) and to note their triggers, subconscious chatter and fears associated with the grief experience.

All with the understanding that as life is to death, so death is to life, and this *is* the human experience common to man. Therefore, we mustn't get **stuck** in the season of grief. Some want to know "*how do I just get over this?*!!!" You don't! You learn to "***get on*** *with it.*" Herein lies the answer to the question "how?"

Chapter 1

Getting to Know Joshua

When Joshua was born to us, beautiful, healthy, and whole, I had no idea of the capacity of the power of love. My heart exploded with joy and I felt like the universe itself was at one with me in the birthing of this being. Remembering that this person was conceived in the purest form of unadulterated love, the love between young lovers, the kind of love that one knows comes from the desire and passion of two finding their oneness. I remember the first day I felt him move in my womb like it was yesterday.

This was the substance of this soul's incarnation. Joshua was born strong, and relatively healthy, except for being a little jaundiced and some stress caused by the fact my pelvis was too small for a vaginal birth. He was a cone-head baby for sure, having gotten stuck in the birth canal. The Lamaze classes were all in vain, the emergency C-section stole my glory! However, we had a handsome baby boy that came out raising his head up and turning toward his Dad as he heard his voice outside of the womb for the first time!

Home with Joshua, and getting used to this little precious life replete with cloth diapers, breastfeedings, and sleep deprivation as I worked to train him to our sleeping pattern consumed my energy. On top of healing from the c-section and the daily care for his needs, I would spend hours holding and looking at how perfect he was. Every inch of him was beautiful, born six pounds and fourteen ounces, twenty-two inches long, every suckle upon my breast was a miracle! The sound of his breaths and of course, that newborn smell, this was my heaven. When his father would come home from work, he would just look at me and shake his head because he knew my entire day had been filled with loving his son. These were some of the most precious moments in my life.

Of course, the days with Joshua turned into years and that first year was remarkable. He was the focus of our lives and everything he did was astonishing to us. A healthy rambunctious boy, he was all boy... curious, explorative, and always moving. Joshua wasn't a "cuddle-bug" per se, but he was affectionate on his terms. I remember introducing foods to him and seeing him look into my eyes searching to find my reasoning for putting the pureed tasteless green beans or peas in his mouth was always funny! He would look at me like.. "You know this is nasty, why are you giving me this?" His expressions were priceless. No amount of applesauce or pears could mask it and he wasn't impressed, but he complied. And that was Joshua, not much fuss, but a heart to please. His favorite was breakfast, never had a problem there! Pureed bananas and either rice or oatmeal would definitely be a clean bowl.

In my culture, a "Fat" or "Juicy" baby is a healthy baby. As early as two months old, a baby would be given "cereal bottles" of breastmilk or formula with at least a tablespoon or two of dried rice cereal in it with a nipple cut large enough to let the thick substance flow controllably free of clogs. Baby, now fed, well burped complete with a clean, dried powdered bottom, would be laid stomach down for digestive support and expected to sleep through the night or nap. At this rate, weight gain is inevitable, yes?! Yes!

Following my cultural norms, I was certain Joshua would develop to be a "Juicy" baby! Not! My mother was convinced that I wasn't feeding him, that I was one of those "young mothers". I was feeling like a failure simply because he wasn't a "juicy" baby! Forget the fact that he was a healthy baby! He wasn't "Juicy" because he was busy!!! Joshua was one of the most active little boys ever! His metabolism was off the charts! He was the kind of child that if you could get in him still long enough, he would relax and go to sleep on the spot. The challenge was... getting him still. Car rides were the best form of soothing him to sleep. Yes, we were those parents loading up the car seat, especially on summer evenings, near bedtime who'd ride around the neighborhood, or take a night's run to the neighborhood mini-mart to get this precious cargo to sleep for the night's rest. Lol!

As Joshua grew, we found ourselves so proud and looking forward to his development and growth. From preschool, to home school, private Christian schools, and graduation from the township school, we found the experiences during his educational process and extracurricular activities one of commitment, determination, and dedication. Joshua tried out for football but found his best pursuits in track and field a better fit. He grew strong and muscular, somewhat lanky and lean, but he was coming into himself and into manhood.

Chapter 2

Know Thyself, The Key to Motherhood

As I reflect over our lives when we were a family, it really was something made of "Leave It To Beaver." I was blessed and loved by my then-husband, to be a stay-at-home mother. Having no real idea of what that meant, I patterned my life after the women around me, the "church ladies". In my family growing up, women didn't stay at home with their children, they worked. Being from a working-class community, all the mother's worked. Those that didn't work either were retired, on disability, welfare, or was the community babysitter for the mothers that did work. But to *choose* not to work and raise your family, well, I didn't have many examples of that in my family or community.

As I shared in the preface, I've always been a different kinda duck! The church was a home away from home for me. It was the place that resonated with my soul. The lively music and the powerful preaching of Dr. James Spencer Wells, truly a man of God's choosing, formed my world view on life in my developmental years. Zion Hope Independent Baptist Church was where I was "saved" baptized, married, and dedicated our children to God's covering. Those formative years of Christian love and devotion to God and my church family were some of the most spiritual and psychological impressionable years of my foundation. My spiritual acuity was well beyond my years. I was often referred to as the "Little Revelator" by my church elders and teachers. My love for God and His word was undeniable. I was always such a serious little person. Deeply sensitive about things, I found the church house to be the place where such expressions of elated joys, shoutings, moanings over "sin", repentance for sin, praising, and testifying about the goodness of the Lord was a haven for me.

In my family's birth order, I am number five of the union between my mother and father. By the time I was almost two, my parents divorced and I remained the "baby of the family" until my mother's second marriage, giving us a beautiful baby sister, number six.

My mother is my Shero, she is one of the strongest people I know. What I mean is, life hasn't been easy for her, but she maintained her family and in her words... "I'm not going in the gutter for nobody, under no circumstances." She meant that!

As a personality, I would liken myself to "Tigger", Winnie The Pooh's side-kick, and my mother to Eeyore. As a child, I had no way to understand the psychological dysfunctions of people suffering from PTSD, Post Traumatic Slave Disorder, we just lived it for generations and are still living it. When you're a child, it's amazing what the little brain does in feeling that somehow that an innocent little one is responsible for the happiness, sadness, or rage surrounding them. This was me. I was considered "sensitive" "too emotional" and a "drama queen". But intuitively I knew when my mother was going to have a "bad day" a "bad week" or "weekend" in most cases. Add to that, the social constructs of Post Traumatic Slave Syndrome, which is slightly different and the disorder itself, *we have such terminology now,* (*I highly recommend Dr. Joy Degure's scholarly works to learn more on the subject*), my mother is a survivor of trauma, indeed.

In my adult years, I have come to understand my mother better and why my life was experienced as it was with her. You see, my mother was my first impression. An example of a grief-stricken, soul-traumatized, never dealt with, unresolved **"stuck"** in a bundle of pain, she was my model.

Her pain and trauma, masked by a tough exterior of "*I'm not taking shit off of anybody and you better damn well not try me!*" was worn like armor. As was her pain and trauma which defined her life. This was my mother's demeanor. But, she could love and support you by making sure you had a roof over your head and you ate every day, but she didn't sugarcoat anything.

Can you imagine having a baby such as me, coming out of the womb singing happily and full of joy and your life is an emotional wreck! I will suffice to say, my mother's life was a life full of potential, but was derailed from its fullest manifestation due to being "**stuck**". I am in no way being disrespectful to my mother, or judgmental, but rather I have an objective assessment of my own life, because in many ways although for years I couldn't see it, I had to admit it I am her. Understanding the environments of our formative years is key to understanding the self. My mother's battles with depression, grief, loss, anger, a sense of powerlessness, yet being powerful was not an easy feat. Her many accomplishments in life were overshadowed by the grief and trauma she experienced. The self-sabotaging grief and trauma that defined her.

An only child, and at the age of eighteen or nineteen, her mother dies rather suddenly. A child bride at sixteen, due to an unplanned pregnancy (in those days you got pregnant, you got married); and the trauma of a stillbirth (a boy) in the midst of a turbulent marriage and all this in the wake of the most devastating pain that to this date still identifies her... the death of her mother, my grandmother Jessie.

As family lore goes, my mother, my grandmother's only child was doted upon as an only beloved child would. Although I'm told my grandmother was stern, my mother was "spoiled". My mother would often say during her binges and wrestlings with her grief, "my mother was my best friend." Now, in context, I'm a child of what, three or four? I'm seeing my mother crying and grieving over her mother whom I'd never met. I would sit before my mother wiping her tears, and wonder, why would this woman, my grandmother, do this to her daughter? At that age, I had no concept of death and the circumstances that surround it. I just knew my momma was sad, and she was sad a lot.

Growing up in a home with a functional alcoholic mother was very stressful as it would be with anyone addicted or suffering from grief, depression, or mental illness. The problem was that back in the day you didn't deal with anything, you just got up and kept going. (Another repercussion of slavery). In my upbringing, crying was a sign of weakness and nobody was going to deal with you being a "crybaby". Even society supports the notion, "Laugh and the world laughs with you. Cry and you'll cry alone." So, in the privacy of her home with J&B Whiskey, Old Forester Bourbon, or Old Granddad Bourbon my mother would grieve, as many people do when there's no place to put the pain.

For many, many years she grieved, and as I grew older and the binges continued. They were often triggered by something in her current state of affairs, but inevitably, it would *always* come back to the death of her mother, mistreatment by her grandmother, and the subsequent traumas from the choices she had made in her life. As a teen and young adult, listening and conversing with my mother, I found I was still that four-year-old child trying to comfort my mother and make her laugh so that she wouldn't be sad and I wouldn't be stressed out and anxious.

I have what I know now as "learned depression". I learned how to suppress and mask my grief, sadness, disappointments, and pains through a vibrant personality and by being a gifted singer. *I am* a drama queen! Lol! I've long belonged on someone's stage, but the DNA of my upbringing and emotional imprint has often caused me to self-sabotage and miss out on truly vibrant life experiences and opportunities. Don't get me wrong, I have had a beautiful life to the point of this writing. However, I think how much more I could have experienced had I understood and known myself as I do today. To this day, my mother is still defined by her grief and embittered by her life experiences, although to meet her, *you* would never know it.

Experiencing my mother as I did, drove me to hide my pain in my optimism and zeal for life! By nature, I am a pretty upbeat person, a true "Sanguine" on the personality charts. Sometimes I can be so optimistic that I get on my own nerves! Lol! But that's me, my mother, sisters, and brother were **not** like me at all. Melancholy would be the description I would use to describe the tenor in our home. There was a constant undercurrent of "dis-ease" in our space. One could never get too excited or be too happy for too long because invariably, the proverbial "shoe" was going to drop.

Which meant, the next crisis was just around the corner and so was the emotional turmoil which led to the drinking binges, verbal abuse and tirades.

At some point, you just learn to function in dysfunction. You learn through the adults around you that gather at holidays or funerals, where *we love each other but as soon as the liquor comes out, we're gonna cuss, fuss, and fight like we ain't kin*, because I remember what you said fifty years ago! Or, "I ain't never liked you or your momma!" or

"I don't know why you married that bum anyway. He ain't nuthin' but breath and britches!" Okay, that might be a bit of an exaggeration, maybe not *every* gathering, but you get my point. The discord and dysfunction was such a fabric of our lives that it was "normal". We only saw or heard the depth of our elder's pain when they drank. Sobriety was reserved for daily survival to ensure jobs were kept and the family was provided for. There was no time to "feel", only time enough to keep going.

Since those years, I have grown and am growing to understand myself through the lens of my mother's eyes. When we fully mature to the understanding that "No man is my enemy, no man is my friend, but every man is my teacher", quoting Florence Scovel Schinn, *The Game of Life and How to Play it* we can then release the people who have hurt us or irritate us. Why, because we come to understand that they serve a significant purpose in our emotional and spiritual development. I could say more about this but it will suffice for now.

Parenting, I believe, is one of the hardest jobs in the world and the most dangerous. Dangerous? Yes. Dangerous! If you haven't come to understand the "self" and are acutely attuned to Spirit and are living an expressed life from spirit, you are simply repeating and perpetuating dysfunction and disease.

Hence, our lives and the lives of our children and grandchildren and the many generations of humanity have suffered, being disconnected from Spirit and living out from a carnal or rather soul-life vs a spirit-life.

When our "Souls", the seat of our emotions and psychological imprinting, is damaged from pre-birth through birth and thereafter, we suffer. The emotional and mental state of a woman when she carries life within her is so beyond valuable that there's no way to quantify its worth. That developing life within her is formed at a cellular level and the DNA transference of generations past and present to make its imprint on that innocent and delicate impressionable being. Some circles refer to this as "generational curses"; the scientific community calls it "cognitive mapping" or "Spatial Use". Much like genetic mapping which identifies the physical markers or imprint of someone, cognitive mapping identifies our emotional markers or imprints.

My Lesson

In this process of thinking about knowing myself through understanding my mother and my relationship to her, I have learned that everything I am, I have learned through the environment of my upbringing. Even in the environment of my mother's womb. My perceptions and my approaches to life were all shaped in my developmental and formative years. The anxiety and battles of insecurity and bouts with depression were all learned and perceived as "normal". The saying... "The struggle is real" is so true.

The only difference between me and my mother is spirituality. I chose, not quite sure just how, but, I believe my intuition or divine nature within fought to live! Not just live, but to thrive! I can truly say that as a child, I was peculiar and I did dream, "see", and "know" things. Just how I knew, not *believed*, but **knew** things, was always a mystery until now. The evolution of the spirit-man is one of the most profound expressions of divinity there is. Having lived long enough to actualize this for myself has changed me in unexplainable ways. To be equipped with the language to contextualize my soul's journey is truly empowering.

The redemptive measure found in the transition of my firstborn son, is that it has created a deep and lasting impressionable "soul-trauma" that has inextricably changed me forever at a cellular level. Dr. Caroline Leaf, a renowned neuroscientist, has done extensive research and work on the brain as a processor and has only confirmed what's been written long ago... "As a man thinks, so he becomes." I found redemption in his transition when I changed the way I thought about it. I found the Grace for my Grief.

Motherhood, womanhood is such an honorable position in this human existence. As a stay-at-home Mom, I used to say, "Motherhood is a proud profession". As a function within the species to carry forth life to the sustaining of humanity is way deeper than childhood dreams of being a mommy and imaginations of "And they lived happily ever after!"

To be a mother-goddess of life, to be healthy enough both spiritually and physically is such a high calling. To do the interior work, or shadow work of the soul BEFORE getting pregnant is just as important as getting physically in shape. Being haphazard about bringing a life into this realm is irresponsible. It is a sacred, major responsibility and should be regarded as such. We have evolved as a species and should no longer perpetuate the dysfunctions from generations past which serve to weaken our existence. What's the saying... "To know better, is to do better"? It's time we started "BEing" better and the doing will come.

I had no idea!!! Do you hear me??? I had no idea of the magnitude of my position and purpose in the earth until I birthed my son back into eternal Spirit. The full circle of his life, meaning I was at the funeral home on the very same day and around the very same time that I gave birth to him into this realm. Viewing the shell which housed his beautiful spirit caused me to KNOW there is a season for all things and a time under heaven. I was chosen to know this most grievous expression of the human experience, the death of a beloved child. If for nothing more than to write this book; to realize the sheer privilege of motherhood. To share with you the reader to know that there is life beyond trauma. If you're reading this book and you know this kind of grief, know this... it all serves a purpose in the evolution of you.

Come, continue with me on my journey of... "The Evolution of Evelyn Rai"!

Chapter 3

Sittin' in "IT"

November 17, 2014, was a Monday a day I will always remember. On that day, sitting on my couch, the spirit of grief was so heavy, you could cut it with a knife. Not only had I buried my firstborn just two days prior, but that day I received the most powerful download of understanding I had ever received throughout the experience.

The death of something, a dream, a marriage, a business or a career is a death that has to be grieved. A void is left and the emptiness of it is felt deeply. When the twenty-five-year marriage to the one human I had vowed to love and devote my life to ended in a pool of delusion and disappointment, I had to learn to "BREATHE" again. This writing isn't about that death experience, but I will suffice to say that what I thought would kill me didn't. I didn't "get over it", but I did "get on with it." Although going through that experience I did not have the verbiage and context that I do now, I sat in it for eight years. I experienced every bit of the "Grief to Grace" journey.

On this Monday, just sitting on my couch the weight of the reality that my Joshua was "**DEAD**!!!" felt like a ton of bricks on my chest! I couldn't breathe. The surreal feelings that I had just buried him, we had the funeral, I was in the limousine all felt like a dream. I wanted it to be a dream. I was alone in my apartment raw and stricken with unbearable pain. Tsunami waves of grief washed over me and took me flat out! The uncontrollable wailings from some place so deep within me were unpredictable and unsettling. From within me I would be screaming, "Why God?! Whyyy???!"

To understand the magnitude of the weight of this grief, I want to share just what I was going through. I've purposefully changed the names of the individuals I reference out of respect for them. You see on July 25, 2014, my dear friend and coworker, I'll call her Allicia Joy, A.J. for short, committed suicide. But even before that, my familia ties to people not of my bloodline but as close to me as kin, we had been trying to wrap our brains around several "Why" questions.

Why, in the summer of 2012 was our beloved Andrew, twenty-four years old, like a nephew to me, murdered as he diplomatically confronted another young man to ask questions about the mistreatment of his dog. We simply wanted to know "why?"

But before we could digest that, in this same family two months later, *why* did the mother of my covenant sister Lucy, our beloved Loraine, aka "Granny" lose her battle to sarcoidosis after a long fight of faith. Watching my sister face these losses, Andrew, actually her first cousin, whom she cared for like her own children and now her mother just months apart in the same year, 2012 was not kind. Not to mention that Lucy was now without mother, father, or sister all who preceded her in death. I watched my friend power through the weight of it all with the conviction and faith of having one's spirit in true alignment with her Creator, God Most High. I marveled at her strength and courage as she supported those grief-stricken family members and friends that surrounded her.

But nothing and I mean NOTHING could have prepared us for what would come just seven months after laying her mother to rest.

Why in May of 2013, when the late night/ early morning call came from Lucy's daughter Elana, my god-niece, telling me that her baby brother Demetrius and his friend had been found murdered in a car, my brain could NOT comprehend what she was saying though sobs and moans. "What?! What?! Elana, what are you saying???" "Where's your mother???" as I jump out of bed to get dressed to get to my family, my brain cannot take in what I'm being told.

Arriving at her parent's house, along with other family members we're all in a state of shock! Demetrius is our baby! The child I witnessed literally come out of his mother's matrix in natural childbirth! He's DEAD?!!! No, this can't be! He's our Demetrius, our "Dare-dare"! Our quiet "don't bother nobody" Demetrius! Our baby, sent to repair the breach! He's only twenty years old God!!! He's in college, he's working a good job! DEAD???! Whyyyy???!!! The story and reasons of his death and the death of his friend murdered by another young black male, another mother's son, is too senseless and egregious to recount.

The point is I found myself in this vortex of grief, shock and disbelief with my sister-girl! One of the most spirit-filled, God-loving, hilariously funny and sanctified women I know. My spiritual mentor and chief friend! In fact, when she found out about her son having been murdered, she was serving at a spiritual retreat in support of those seeking a deeper walk and connection with the Creator! She wasn't at a nightclub or giving herself to mindless self-indulgences, she was serving her fellow man in service to God! Are you kidding me right now???!

I was beyond bewildered. We were raw, and had to get through yet another funeral. We had barely processed Andrew and Loraine and now Demetrius!!! The effects of these repeated instances of soul-traumas had taken its toll on us and our children and the fathers.

Lucy, a mother of four and me, a mother of two, and raising my sister's daughter like my own, watched helplessly as our children and their circle of friends all began to spiral downward. We had raised our children together. We are interconnected. Our children all flowed in some of the same circles. There were birthday parties, cookouts, graduations, church gatherings and holidays and Sunday dinners. Friends and extended family members alike, we all began to walk around in this daze of despair. Shaking our heads, wanting this season to make sense. When we looked into each other's eyes, there was this unspoken exchange: why is this happening? Everything was happening too fast. We were having family viewings of the remains of our loved ones, graveside rituals and repast dinners all without time to process the weight of this pain and the sense of loss. All without the time to just "Sit IN it"!!!

I had just moved back to town in 2012, after taking a job in Detroit. Initially, I relocated to Atlanta following the death of my twenty-five-year marriage. I was facing life with my "Big Girl Panties" on. A clear ending and a new beginning. I was just learning to "get on" with "it". Now... Here I was, back in my hometown, experiencing the deaths of loved ones, with an eerily familiarness in my psyche. Meaning, I'm feeling the same emotions I felt when I had to process the season marking the end of my marriage.... This was GRIEF, again! But with this season came something we could not speak out loud... An overwhelming sense of anxiety. We were truly scared! This was not normal.

This backstory was necessary to share because I had to process all this pain, when once again who knew??? Like how NOTHING, again, could have prepared me, prepared us, for yet another soul-trauma on November 8, 2014. By now, we just can't... we can't connect or gather together. As parents, we're trying to grasp the strength and language to explain to our grandchildren and children "why" when in fact, we're seeking to understand ourselves. From January 2014 to December of 2015, I went to over fifteen funerals of family members and friends. Then I just stopped! I couldn't go to not another single one.

Looking back on that particular Monday, November 17, 2014, I got "it"! A.J. (Alicia Joy) had left me traumatized and bewildered by her choice to end her life as she did. Sittin' IN "it" on my couch, I knew exactly why she did what she did. My well-meaning, best-intended, sanctified life had not shielded me from all this grief and sorrow. Bad things do happen to innocent, decent people. I didn't say perfect people, I said innocent human beings. In that moment on the couch, I just wanted to die! It was enough, and with this new looming sense of anxiety, I'm freaking out about my living children and grandchildren and extended family and friends. Now, before you judge me as... but I thought you were a Believer in God or I thought you were a leader in your faith. What I'm conveying has little to do with religious practices, roles and rituals but more about what makes us human and how those practices, roles and rituals play a part in processing the very natural and human experiences of trauma, grief and the sense of loss.

We all know that unless you have experienced something, you cannot speak to it firsthand. A. J. took her life because it seems that for years she had been carrying the grief of having lost her only son Matthew, and within a year after his death, his baby girl died after the result of a fall. Can you imagine? Her only grandchild and her only connection to her son is gone too. I get it! Life can be bitter! That was a bitter blow for her. Sittin' IN it, I'm on the couch begging Abba to take me, when within my being I hear, that's why she crossed your path! OMG! Right in the middle of deep grief and anguish, here was a "Why" being answered. It had been at least SIXTEEN years or more that she carried that pain inside. It destroyed her! Her family relations and all her relationships had suffered.

You see, I hadn't known A.J. for a very long time, a little over nine months to be exact. We were coworkers at a company and we just clicked in a highly stressful environment. Making the time pass by singing show tunes, speaking in characters of Irish, British, and Jamaican, accents. She was such a beautiful spirit! A true "Flower-Child"! Hilariously witty, a bad-a$$, cook like a black woman cook! And yet beneath all that I saw her! I felt her. I knew her. I knew she was in a lot of pain. We had *lost* Andrew and Demetrius, so when she brought in cookies to share with us commemorating the deaths of her son and granddaughter, I respected that and honored her by partaking of her most delicious treats. I listened to her stories. I went home with her once when she was having an emotional meltdown trying to hold it all together with this gaping void hole in her heart and soul. I loved her with all the Christ Love I had inside me. At the end of our evening together, she thanked me for, as she put it, "bringing her back to her Big Brother Jesus" and for saving her life. She mentioned to a friend who came to pick me up from near downtown where she lived, when she said, "She saved my life tonight." I chuckled uncomfortably and said "J, stop it!" She looked me dead in the eyes with a chilling directness. I dismissed it. I invited her out to my apartment and we cooked out and ate together. Laughed and sang, but always that deep undercurrent of pain could be felt. She came to one of my shows. I just knew she would be all right, *we* would get through this together..., not so. She did it...She planned it and set herself free. And, just like that she was gone! I was devastated! I wasn't there for her. I fought guilt and once again, anxiety took over.

She'd left her suicide letter addressed to me. She'd left me her most precious possessions. I found myself leading the band as fellow coworkers and I planned her memorial service and liquidated her estate. It seemed that she had estranged herself from siblings due to her mental health issues precipitated, if not exacerbated undoubtedly by the weight of her grief. This resourceful, loving spirit was gone. But I understood her that day sittin' in it on my couch. I hadn't understood much of why I had been going through, but in that moment of "Sittin' IN 'It'", I found the key that unlocked the question to "where do I put this pain, this emptiness?" My beloved A.J. had nowhere to put it.

The pharmaceutical companies can drug you into dependency, creating a false sense of stability that allows one to function well enough to labor in the cog of society. But they cannot manufacture a drug that can give solace and comfort to the soul and spirit. In retrospect, I believe she agreed to come to this plane to teach me a lesson in a chapter of my life with grief. Knowing that A.J. was sent to teach me, brought her death and transition into perspective. It took the sting out of it. She was my example to teach me, to remind me that I do possess a living hope. That I do have a place, and someone to take on the weight of my grief. Someone willing, for as long as it takes, to just "Sit IN 'It'" with me. That I have a choice what I will do with the pain.

Chapter 4

Walking with Grief and Grace

This revelation marked the beginning of my journey in moving from Grief to Grace. I had made it through Joshua's *"Celebration of Life"* service, the gravesite and now I sat on my couch processing this newly downloaded information. I could not continue to cry out for death to come claim me, I had been given new enlightenment and understanding. But even with that, I was broken and still in despair. I had been armed with the knowledge that I would survive, and that I could survive this, but the issue was... wanting to! I didn't want to. How do you look Hope in the face and say... yeah, thanks but no thanks!? It wasn't a "God" problem or even a "Faith" problem. It wasn't a "Scripture" problem but it was a very human problem. The matter of a traumatized soul.

Every day for many days after November 17, 2014, sittin' IN **it** was all I could do. My mind couldn't stop replaying all of the scenarios and scenes of my beautiful son laid out on the examining table, butchered from being autopsied. At the hospital, we weren't even allowed to touch him. My next physical encounter with him was at the mortuary on his birthday. He was cold and hard, I knew he wasn't in that avatar, but that avatar was everything that represented him to me. I had watched it grow and develop. I had carried it within my body, and now here it lay stretched out in front of me lifeless and cold. These are the scenes that ran continuously in my mind. Bursting in like an assailant on my sanity. The tsunami waves of grief were so unpredictable. The searing ache in my heart (physically) and my soul was at times unbearable. Even with the comfort and presence of the Holy Spirit, armed with the knowledge that I am being made to understand some of life's most difficult lessons, nothing and I mean nothing blunted the pain I was experiencing. Of course my family and friends grew concerned. And I had no strength to fight. Me! Queen Optimistic was lower than low. I kept asking during that time "what's the point?" Life had been good before. I had known love, marriage, family, traveled to other countries and experienced to some degree, "the American Dream". But this season... this season right here??? Like, what did I *do* to deserve this? God, are You angry with me? I mean, I don't understand. I had to get still. In my stillness, I got real acquainted with my flesh, the natural part of me. My doctor wanted to put me on the same antidepressant that A.J. was on, one of the side effects was not only confusion, but suicide. Are you kidding me???!

Even though I wanted to die, taking my life, I knew, wasn't for me to do. I had already experienced the trauma of my eldest sister having made her decision to do that when I was in the third grade, her leaving two beautiful baby boys behind. I know what that decision did to my mother and the rest of us. Nah... I couldn't do that, but the idea of going to sleep and never waking up again on this side really appealed to me. Come to think about it, I believe that's why A.J.'s choice landed on me the way that it had, it was such a deep and familiar pain.

While I sat many days just staring into space, it was like every grief I'd ever known sat in it with me. I was so raw and numb that I was wondering if I was having a nervous breakdown. Every emotion was magnified times one hundred! During this season of grief, just after committing Joshua's remains to the grave, the traditional holidays of Thanksgiving and Christmas were upon us. We had a small birthday gathering that evening of November 14th at the apartment. It was weird, but I had to in some way reach for something positive because the next day would be his funeral. It all had been so surreal. And the holidays were mournful. I let them pass. I wasn't interested.

I remember the days right after Josh's passing, not being able to breathe. It was like, I just couldn't catch my breath or breathe in enough air. I was panting and would have to tell myself... "breathe,

Evelyn, just breathe". I would breathe and then right behind that breath, the tears would flow again. I could feel two very strong presence with me now. They were new in my energy sphere. It was like my Guardian Angels were still around, but more like in the shadows instead of with me. Since they are assigned to me, any distinction of separation felt is a sign that something is out of alignment. I was so out of alignment, but I noticed these new unfamiliar entities. So I asked Abba (God) who they were, and it was revealed that it was Grief and Grace. One morning coming out of sleep, but not quite fully awake, I sensed them so vividly. Grief was sitting in this chair that I had next to my bed and Grace was standing at the foot of my bed. Both of them were very "supportive". I know this sounds weird, but it's the best way to describe the experience.

In my understanding, having been told I would have to know this pain of trauma and that it would serve a purpose in my life, I was given the gifts of these entities to accompany me along the way. On some mornings, I would begin the day walking with Grace, courageously facing the challenges of each moment with its strength supporting me. But by the time the day or moment ended, Grief would be right there embracing me with such care. As strange as it may sound, walking with these two entities was comforting because they each served a purpose and I knew instinctively that they were necessary in the process of this human being utilizing these experiences in a natural and healthy way. I really wasn't living day by day, I was living moment by moment.

In this age of artificial foods and virtual realities, when you begin to speak of real spiritual encounters with the divine, people tend to look at you side-eyed. However, throughout scripture we see angels or divine beings interacting with human beings. And since from my childhood, such encounters were more frequent and I was more attuned to spirit as a child, I wasn't too disturbed by their presence. My new companions, although not physical, were very prevalent. I could tell when Grief and I were going to have extensive times of interactions, because I was in a constant battle with myself. I was dying yet another death... the death of the ego, of the self. Grace, in all of its glory would be right there to lift me up from the stench of sorrow and woe and clean me up moment by moment, reminding me of God's unconditional love for me and my access to it. Grace like Grief was a faithful companion, patiently giving me what I needed to get through each moment. This was in fact going to be a journey with no clear destination in sight. I just had to trust I would make it through to the otherside.

I began to isolate myself because I couldn't take the interactions of others. Emotionally I was too raw still, and everything, and I do mean everything seemed to be magnified as a crisis. Even normal things which wouldn't ordinarily bother me bothered me extremely. I believe that in that state of mind I was psychologically imbalanced.

I didn't want people to be uncomfortable with my grief as I was. I knew I wasn't special in this experience, but this was me now... my experience, and I didn't quite know how to "do" grief like this. I didn't even know how to "do" sad, because my natural disposition is so upbeat. Since I had grown up in a home filled with depression, I had made the world I lived in one of lightheartedness, joy and peace. So when this season came upon me, I stayed to myself. Truly I felt like I was in a foreign culture, but somehow it was familiar.

I was in a relationship, a second marriage, but it too was on life support. I knew it was going to die. Here I was sittin' in it, with every definition of who I thought I was, destroyed. Nothing says defeat like a "*failed*" marriage, I now had two, or the death of a child. The self-tauntings, and self-loathings coupled with feelings of failure and deep, deep disappointments covered me like mold on cheese. I was dying emotionally and worse yet, I wanted to. I was living back in the city I'd sworn I would never live in again, stuck in it in despair. And for the second time, my confidence was shot to hell! Talk about a dark night of the soul... It was oh so dark!

With everything in me, for my entire life, I had fought *not* to become my mother's example. Not to turn on myself and become someone that I used to know. I had fought hard not to be the one who began her sentences with "I used to..." but here I was staring me (my mother) right in the face! I had married someone akin to my mother in personality disorder and depression. Of course I did, and why?

Because the spirit was familiar, although masked and hidden, I instinctively knew it which is why I couldn't see it. I had bonded with my mother through her trauma. I had bonded with this person through their trauma. The connection was real, but it was really wrong.

I am an Empath, and my sensitivity to emotions and the energies of others is like a superpower. However, this ability without understanding of the self and the purpose for such a gift can be very costly. I was paying the cost in that relationship, and the truth of it couldn't have been revealed at a worse time. For this person, as dear as they were to me, was incapable of consoling me or caring for me during the deepest psychological, emotional breakdown and heartbreak of my life. I was alone.

Angry, disappointed and devastated by his deception, I *turned on myself* even more for having been in my mind "stupid". Now I couldn't even trust my own decision-making. What was so strange and frightening to me during this time was, **I couldn't hear the music in me anymore!** In my entire existence, I had NEVER not heard music in me... a melody or tune of something, but nothing was thereI couldn't hear the music!!! My anxiety was off the charts and I was in fear! I couldn't read my Bible, devotionals or anything. However, I would listen to the bible, as I went to sleep at night which kept me from utterly losing it altogether.

I began to abuse myself by smoking black and milds, marijuana and drinking strong liquor. These behavior choices of mine were on fertile ground, since I had married a person in whose past had the testimony of the power of God to deliver a person from the ravages of some of the most destructive drugs and lifestyle choices. However, this person's reality of having overcome the most dark and deep situations faced had brought him to the hope of a new life. However, the problems lied in the dark, the shadow work was **not** being done! Meaning, whatever lurks in the shadows of our souls **will** make its way to the forefront of our lives. A "Recovered" hardcore drug addict, by his own admittance for sure, but his functional alcoholism and his habitual marijuana use had become very evident, not a conversation discussed or revealed in the more than six years of building a "friendship".

Therefore, the pressure for him was too much; the arguments were too many. Neither of us liked arguing. I could no longer nurture that which he found needful from me to be supported. I believe he tried to be supportive in the best way that he knew, but he was far too inadequate for my needs, because he hadn't been honestly dealing with his own. He was a cigarette smoker (who told me he could quit anytime he chose to, but he didn't) and so guess what, eventually, I started smoking too. The familiarness of smoking was a family trait. Something that was "normal" in my family. In fact, as a child, I had an aunt who reared foster children...it was a family of girls along with her own and she was a smoker. It was common for her to say to the older girls, "Which one of you heifers is gonna light my cigarette?" When I chose to smoke cannabis, it enabled me to sleep. I didn't particularly like it or the drinking, but I was becoming an insomniac and trying to manage the pain of brokenheartedness and disappointment. The nicotine and the THC (psychoactive cannabis compound) had its calming effects. None of my choices to be unhealthy were his fault, it's just that the environment was conducive for it. It was a setup for the journey I was on. I wanted an escape and to not feel, so such indulgences of unhealthiness are always accommodating. Much like food is a drug for many, emotional eating or whatever the device only leads to more bondage.

Grief, unchecked, becomes bondage. We are such powerful beings, that when we focus on anything without balance and boundaries, we will be consumed by that thing or person. The reality is that such an environment was the makings of what I had grown up in. I had been cultivated in being unhealthy, to turn to substances as a means of coping with disparities, and I had opened the door to all the familiar spirits I had been running from my entire life..., *Subterranean levels being revealed.*

This new marriage was doomed and my hopes of renewed love and life had been shattered. Although he had not become physically violent, the emotional abuse was unbelievable. Our living together had become beyond toxic for me, a ticking time bomb. I have since forgiven him and myself for making such a huge mistake. To his credit, he acknowledged his depression and apologized for not being the husband and friend I needed. I asked his forgiveness for failing to see that I was no match for the past which he continued to grieve and what he needed in a wife. Had I not given myself permission amidst all the shame and reproach of yet another marriage ending in divorce, even the fragile friendship that remains between us wouldn't be intact. Always remembering... **"No man is my enemy; no man is my friend, but every man is my teacher."** I learned many lessons through that experience and season with him which has served in causing me to understand myself *even* more. I thank my friend and I pray for him. Thank you, Abba, for the lessons learned!

During this period, my "dark night of the soul", I was spiraling away, far away from my center and I could only sit in it. My FMLA (Family Medical Leave Act) was ending, I had to get back into this thing called "LIFE". Once I had gone to a grief support group at the encouragement of some staying close to me; but that was worthless for me because of my empathic nature. I came away from the session bearing the grief of those whose stories I'd heard and ironically found myself giving them words of encouragement and praying for them asking God to comfort them and strengthen them and to be with them.

Ain't that crazy?! I'm stuck in my own shit, *excuse my "french" sometimes that is the most apropos word for expression.* But here I am, and can hardly see the light of day, praying for them when I can't get a prayer out for myself. I'm encouraging them when I can't find the courage for myself! I'm praying and encouraging others when I'm not in the least feeling like an ambassador of the Kingdom of God! Which only served to heap more condemnation on me because on top of everything else, I'm feeling like the biggest hypocrite on this side of glory! Like I don't even know what I believe in anymore.

I'm like how can I be saying these things? Before the FMLA completely ran out, and I had to go back to work, I tried to seek help again. After all, I'm a trained bible counselor having over thirty years of ministry experience. Riiight! I was jacked up! I know I was jacked up. I know jacked up when I see it and I was totally jacked! Did I mention I was jacked up?! SMH (shaking my head in disbelief)!

I was never a pretender or fake in my walk as a Christian. I took the ministry and calling seriously, which was another reason for such despair, I found myself in a place I had not known about myself! As one of my spiritual mothers, "Mother Love", would say... "Girl, you've got subterranean levels about you that you don't even know yet." She was so right. In my sessions with the counselor, it was like I just needed a safe place to say what I felt without feeling judged or further condemned. She was a good listener, but she just smiled and said, "I believe you know what to do, you just need the courage to do it; to do what will be in the best interest of your mental health and in alignment with your soul's spirituality". Basically, she knew she was listening to someone that could identify their issues. Someone who has a solid foundation of morals and values, but found themselves overwhelmed from being in an extended season of grief and trauma having dealt with many disappointments in her life. The sessions ended well; I needed a safe place to just **BE**.

Unable to keep my beautiful apartment and still having to function to keep a roof over my head, manage the responsibilities of maintaining day to day, I went to work for temp agencies, but I just couldn't handle it. For the first time in my life I was "fired"! Another blow, it was very politely done, they told the agency to find someone else more capable for the work environment. My grief was obvious even with the corporate look and articulate vernacular I wasn't fooling too many. Besides, I was exhausted, just getting out of bed was a chore, not to mention learning new systems and procedures. I was totally overwhelmed which led to more drinking and smoking, which led to more depression and the cycle I saw in my mother was beginning to take its hold on me, I freaked out! Needless to say many things came to an end that subsequent year following Joshua's transition. The marriage, the job(s) and all my illusions of myself's definitions of me in this experience called life, died.

Sittin' IN it with Grief and Grace was painful and foreign. Who was I now? I didn't even recognize myself. Beloved trusted friends and some family were careful with me. Some knew the grief I'd become so acquainted with, and others not so much, but yet loved me and just wanted Evelyn back. Heck! I wanted her back too, but she was gone... she had been irrevocably changed. The season of grief was evident and I had to adjust. Do you know what it's like when you don't even recognize yourself anymore??? I'll tell you, Scary as Hell!

I had to move to a new residence. Surely a change from the environment which held all the reminders of the traumas from the last twelve months would be good. The reality wasn't what I had expected. Relocation back down into the city from the suburbs was an outward manifestation of how I felt within. I moved into a rental in a depressed area of town. Although slated for gentrification and the signs of if had begun, the money hadn't quite made it to the particular block I'd moved on. But that one block was one of the cleanest and the multi-family dwelling in which I lived was nice. I was grateful, but I didn't realize how bougie I was until I moved just south of west 38th street, in the "inner-city". The blatant drug deals, homeless people, poverty and constant police surveillance was an eye opener. A far cry from my culdesac communities, gated complex suburban lifestyle communities I'd known.

A depressed, middle-aged single woman in such a neighborhood, now this was going to be interesting. Anxious about the new community, I bought a security system with a camera on the doorbell and a camera in the backyard. With permission from the Landlord, I had motion-sensored lighting in the backyard; and from a breeder, I purchased a beautiful purebred German Shepherd, "King Solomon Haus", bringing him home at only eight weeks old; a true K9 quality dog. He is such a good companion and a fierce protector. I needed a dog for the sense of protection, but also to focus on something other than my grief and depression. He was the key, his demands to be trained, exercised and to play got me out of the bed and out of the house. I not only had him, but I also bought a cat. The house hadn't been lived in for a while and it sat off the alley of a vacant lot, so you know I was having all kinds of meltdowns when the reality of "Jerry" (mice) or "Jerrys" became evident. Yes ma'am... went right out and got me a cat! "Tom and Jerry" had now become live and in living color. The landlord had been responsible for putting bait down, but these mice were smart and knew the ropes. My "little kitten boy" "Messiah Moses", was the sweetest, tiniest little thing only eight weeks by estimate. I adopted him from the humane society complete with vaccinations, neutered and papers. I had never owned a cat before and that first night was interesting. He was separated from his mother too early...I'll have to tell you that story another time. But there I was with my new little family of "fur babies", my "puppy boy" and my "kitten boy", *my* grief and *my* depression. *My* disappointment, *my* bitterness and *my* pain.

It's two years after Josh's death and transition and I'm desperately trying to hold it together because God Himself has made it perfectly clear, "You're going to go from grief to grace." Sitting IN it, in my new environment, I manifested all of the negative energies swirling within. Feelings of unworth and defeat was the chatter which played continuously in the background of my subconsciousness. Even though I had moments of clarity to survive, I was still sinking in the mire of my pain, bobbing up enough not to drown in it. This grief was real. I had given up so much spiritual and personal ground, but something within was fighting, fighting to survive. I was. The real me yet to be revealed to me was fighting. That girl was NOT going down!

"EVERYTHING has a season... Don't get stuck in any particular one"

My Lesson:

Growth and transition comes in stages, nothing grows overnight. Nothing grows without dying first. Letting go of people and things which cannot serve to enable us to become the best and highest version of ourselves is not only a wise thing to do, it is the healthiest form of love. Honest, transparent and harmonious Love for self, for the other person or the overall situation. I had let go of an unhealthy marriage, which was another type of "death" and many relationships shifted during that time too, some of which have not recovered because I recognized the season for them was over. Another type of "death".

In a new season, the new community where I lived, I became acutely aware of daily painful realities of being identified with a class of people suffering the effects of mental illness, systemic racism, inequities, food deserts and needless poverty. Living among my people brought me to a state of awareness that I'd long forgotten, while in my personal pursuits for "success" and the "American Night-terror aka 'Dream'". I had forgotten about loving my neighbor, just as I had forgotten about loving me. I had even lost sight of my neighbor, just as I had lost sight of me. Seeing the fragile community in all its dysfunction, made me reminisce of childhood days gone by when we as a people cared for and sincerely loved one another. When the first thing you'd hear from "Auntie" or "Big Momma", "You hungry?" When rent parties were thrown because we didn't wanna see family put out in the streets, because they'd invariably suffered a malady or an injustice of some kind. When our fathers and uncles gathered over early morning fishing trips and we neighborhood children scrambled to catch nightcrawlers to supply them with the bait. A time when if one suffers, we all suffer. A time when, if you got out of line, you'd get two or three chastisements before even reaching your parent's home. The seasons of my life. But..., we'll talk about that another time.

Chapter 5

Dead Yet Alive

Now what God?! What am I supposed to do now? I thought I was Your ambassador, Your minister of truth and the Good News, but look at me! These were my real and truly raw conversations with The Father. They were on a "whole nother level"! I had to figure out my life and just what all this sense of grief, loss and pain meant. What am I to do with this void in my life? It is said, "Let not many of you become teachers, my brethren, knowing that as such we will incur a stricter judgment." (*NASB 1995*)

A gifted teacher, but as I like to say, "facilitator", because the Holy Spirit teaches, I knew by experience and profession that I was called to lead, speak and to motivate. I have these amazing gifts of exhortation, administration and nurturing. I say this by way of observation in how I function and show up in the world, not ego. These are natural abilities that have been honed through disciplines and dedication. I've served on many boards, as executive interim directors, and in leadership as a licensed minister under the christian evangelical auspice. I've been a television anchor, co-anchor and public affairs host for a local affiliate. I've been hired as a motivational speaker and have served at many retreats and conferences. Yet even with such abilities and platforms, the inner-self, that wounded, insecure, emotionally bereft "little girl" was still in there seeking. Lurking in the shadows behind my ego, still underdeveloped and screaming like many others, "What's it all about Alphie?"

That world now seems so distant and strangely behind me. None of those titles inferred upon me matters. None of the pursuits or aspirations means anything. In those days, I needed to know the purpose for my living? Like, for real....why am I here? I had done things the way Christianity says it's to be done. I gave it my all, without a "plan B"! Had I not survived my childhood and teen years. Had I not just gone through a life-changing metamorphosis surviving the divorce after twenty-five years? Had I not just come through learning how to live with myself for the first time? Didn't I take a chance on love again after almost eight years of celibacy wanting to be a wife again, only for it to end twenty-five months later? In my then perception, I was failing at life and failing miserably. I was walking, yet dead inside.

Emotionally fragile, Daddy-God, gave me *time* and *space* to become intimately acquainted with myself to *learn* to love myself the way He loves me... for who I am, not who I thought I was. Not for the positions or roles I played on the stage of life. But greater still, for who He made me to be, which is still being revealed to me at the time of this writing. I'm experiencing a depth of spirituality that is causing me to grasp this deep understanding of... "The **steadfast** love of the Lord **never** ceases; His mercies **never** come to an end; they are new **every** morning; great is Your faithfulness. (Lamentations 3:22-23 ESV) *Bold my emphasis.*

I couldn't believe it... the death experience was working love in me. A greater love. Although I was being flogged by my life! Stripped and naked, bearing my cross, I had to face myself as I was. Broken, weak and powerless, even with all that knowledge of scripture, it was in this season of grief that I came to understand experientially the depth, length and breadth of His "Steadfast Love". Like I said, I love words, especially old ones. Check out the etymology of the word STEADFAST. {*The Old English stedefæst "secure in position, steady, firm in its place," from stede (see stead) + fæst (see fast (adj.)); similar formation in Middle Low German stedevast, Old Norse staðfastr "steadfast, firm; faithful, staunch, firm in one's mind." Of persons, in English, "unshakable, stubborn, resolute" from c. 1200. Related: Steadfastly, steadfastness.*} Resourced from Etymology.com When I understood that my Daddy's love wasn't going anywhere, that it was not conditional. It was not based on merit, I was set free, once again, from a meritorious mentality. Did you read where the definition said unshakeable, stubborn, resolute? I was a trained BAPTIST baby! I knew I wasn't getting into heaven based on any "good works" I'd done! It was going to be GRACE alone! I could quote a scripture right here, but I won't, Lol! Let's just say I'm in the BOOK!

I was born into a world that judges you by your performance, where you're rewarded or shamed based on how someone else's judgment of you is merited. I was subconsciously relating to The Creator as though human. Treating Him like a Daddy of human origin in a relationship gone bad with His daughter. Hadn't I been good Daddy, faithfully walking circumspectly before you? "Circumspect" is one of those bible words! KJV version fo' sho'! You might want to go look it up. But here I was now, "Piti-FUL" in the "Pit" "Full" of my misguided emotions, broken dreams, sad memories and the beauty of all beauties..., He was sittin' right in the "pit" with me! Wow! Talking about steadfast love!

In my process of living this human experience, I had a working knowledge of a lot of scriptures, but it's altogether different when you become one with them. And I've many, many moments of them. What I mean is, times when those "scriptures" or "words" in a book written in ink come to life and breathes into my soul. When something that was penned by the thoughts and inspirations of others becomes actualized in your very being. It hasn't just been the Bible either. I had been privileged to have had hours of study time in the scriptures, dictionaries and commentaries of those deemed "Fathers of the Faith" when I was a stay-at-home mom. As a student of the "Word", courses of study and tools to study God's Word fueled my toolshed. Learning to translate scripture from the Hebrew and Greek text satisfied the hunger in me to know God and to be a true vessel in serving others in His Spirit and in Truth. Not for fame or gain, because I have seen my share of false teachers, manipulating the people for gain. I wanted to be a true one, or not one at all. So often ashamed by those who gave us bible teachers a bad rap, I would seldom speak of my training and found my circle small because I just couldn't stomach the hypocrisy and the fakery! Yet here I was feeling like the biggest "fake" this side of heaven. I was so disappointed by life and my place in it. The life I knew was now dead!

A new community and new relationships being fostered, I was reluctantly being resuscitated to life. During the initial grief season, the only job I could do within the strain of my emotional bandwidth was caregiving, I went back to being a caregiver. A lifelong friend has a wonderful business and we affectionately call her the "Baby Whisperer", she gave me an assignment with several of her clients and I landed with one family exclusively for about a year. Caring for a set of twin boys was just the prescription I needed. The new growing family was such a blessing to me and we bonded quickly. Parents trusting you with their children is something that has to come from intuition. The boys were so sweet and tiny with that newborn smell, I needed to be reminded of life and its preciousness. I began with the family coming in at night training the babies to develop a sleeping pattern and eventually became their caregiver during the day when mom went back to work. These babies grew and thrived under my care. The parents and I joined forces in creating a healthy environment for them. Being in their home, while I tried to figure out my life was the sanctuary I needed.

When I graduated high school as a junior, I had enrolled in nursing school and was accepted, but I also had gotten married right out of high school. So when I found myself unexpectedly pregnant before I began the semester, my then husband wanted me home and I chose not to go to nursing school, but rather to grow and nurture our own family. The decision to forego nursing school would be a tiny regret in my life.

Nevertheless, I found myself with this family, caregiving again as I had done many times over in the seasons in my life. Caring for my grandparents until they transitioned and having worked for agencies as a personal caregiver or home health aid. This family even supported me by being flexible with my hours and substitute coverage as I took a training course to become a certified nursing assistant, (CNA).

"Though he is dead, yet shall he live." I was the living dead, still walking with Grief and Grace. I couldn't deny the power of the Life of the Divine within me fighting for me and with me to survive the season of grief. I would awaken, grateful for my little existence with my fur babies and the fact that I had a roof over my head and I could still take care of myself. Yet, as the season with the family came to a natural end, the boys were going to daycare. I was headed into the world of promotional products sales and marketing; thankful that I have some of the most loving and supportive family and friends ever.

"You shall live and not die!" was the spoken declaration over me, evidenced by having achieved my (CNA) certification, and on top of that, given a new career path in marketing, social media marketing and project managing. This too was nothing I saw on the radar of my life. However, a middle-age blackwoman with a lot of experience but no degrees of completion, reinvention and transition was the order of the day. I had to abandon every concept of who I **thought** I was. Where every notion of what I thought my life was to be had been devastated. I was "humilified" a word made up of "humiliated" and "stupified" combined makes "humilified!" However, I found I wasn't the only one.

So I was learning the art of being "fluid" or "flexible". If the season of grief taught me anything, it taught me to HOLD EVERYTHING LOOSELY and to wear this world as a loose garment. I remember a saying I read once, "Blessed are the flexible, for they shall not be bent out of shape." I had no idea just how prophetic the saying would be in my journey.

During the midst of this new transition in my life, I had two narratives playing in my mind about myself. So much of who this new Evelyn was, had been redefined by her soul trauma with grief. Therefore, that *first narrative* ended up with many of my introductions like, "this is Evelyn, she just lost her son." Or I would introduce myself in such a way that I was wearing my trauma as some type of badge of suffering. Much like some people with mental illnesses or disabilities can tend to do. I get it. I too just wanted people to see me, to see my pain. That I am hurting deeply. My heart is broken. Can't you see that?!

In that first narrative, I was beginning to define my life by the one day that ended the life of my firstborn, as I knew him, rather than the thirty years I had with him. I will never forget my beloved friend Penny saying to me one day, loving and serving me as only she can, she said, "Evelyn, I know you're going to miss Josh, but not longer than you'll be with him again." Her words of that eternal hope fed me that day and for days to come. In essence what she was saying is, we have a living hope. Life in the Divine of God lives on. Basically, energy never dies, it is eternal and continues forth just in another form. The words and the understanding helped in that moment.

But I was still in the "pit of despair" functioning out of necessity, I was getting comfortable in that pit! For all intents and purposes, my life had stopped and I was forced to keep living it. (This was the very beginning of really understanding my mother through these experiences with myself.) Although I had enough sense to be grateful for even the smallest of things, I wasn't keen on living because I could no longer see the point of it. I really didn't could no longer see humanity's overall worth. In this world of corruption, lies, deceit and sheer hypocrisy the masses are subject to the whims of a few controllers. The manipulation of generations of peoples and societies is mind boggling to me. All of the contrived wars and the devastation of such a beautiful planet, our only home, I was beginning to think, God, if You're really, really, real, You got some "splainin" to do! I basically said, "I accept Your offer God, to 'come let us reason together' *Isaiah 1:18, KJV* because this life is NOT making any sense whatsoever." In days to come, He would oblige.

The *second narrative* surrounding my life was the fact that I was alive... and death for me was nowhere to be found! Like a resilient weed, Divine Life kept springing forth, no matter how many rejections and how gross the soil of my emotions, that manure was serving to grow some awesome spiritual fruit, although at the time it stank to high heaven! The fruit *was* budding and I couldn't deny it. At times I really resented it! I was like... "You have the audacity to grow and give hope while everything about me seems hopeless!" Really?!!! Oh, I was a hot mess! Grace upon grace was being poured out on me and I was a bit angry about it. The irony of it made for a bitter taste in the mouth. The power of Divine Grace was placing a demand on my soul, the seat of my emotions and I didn't like it. But that's when I understood that the "resilient weed" was in fact the blooming of a beautiful flower. I learned the story of the Lotus Flower. You should check it out some time! Anyway…. In my emotions, I had a "right" to feel this way, after all, I had experienced the deepest form of grief, yeah?! *Indeed!* And…, I had been twice disappointed by marriage, yeah?! *Indeed!* And, and…, I had been reduced to poverty and scarcity, yeah?! *Indeed!* Well, somebody explain to me what's the meaning of this Divine Life growing within me?! And one day in my inner being, I heard as the Elders would say, "gal, git somewheres and *sat* down!" Lol! not sit down. As if to say on a higher frequency… "Come take your seat where you've sat, because you have forgotten your place." Wow! I had to go within again as I would watch to see what His Spirit would say to me. I'm so glad that my Daddy-God can handle this lil' spitfire He's made because His Steadfast Love is ever present with me! 😊

"Unless a grain of wheat falls… and dies…"

My Lesson

The life I embarked upon from marrying at seventeen years old, the transition of Joshua to my current status of oneness, and everything in between, has been the culmination of many deaths and my response to them. For each death, no matter the type, serves to teach me something about me. Nothing has the potential of purifying the soul like a void, a grief, or a trauma.

For it is in this space where we humans learn of the true nature of the self and our relationship to our life experiences and to The Creator. Truth, as seen in nature, is evident that out of death comes life. Seasons change and things of life evolve. The fertile grounds of death are producing the richness of a well-balanced soul and a rightly aligned divine spirit. The life I was striving for could never have been met by the superficial identities we foster upon ourselves or by others. No, the Divine Life of a Divine Human Being, is forged from depths of human suffering tempered by the power of Divine Love. I've heard it said that

49

"the measure of a man isn't by what he achieves, but rather by what he overcomes".

Grief and Grace had to be my companions during the season of grief. I had to feel every emotion and experience every experience of me no matter how shocking. Nothing was hidden that wouldn't be uncovered and I had to learn patience and acceptance; first to be patient with me and second to truly accept me for me and in the lyrics of John Legend's All of Me, "I love all my perfect imperfections". My grief season of "Sit IN it" ended November 8, 2019, five years to the day of Joshua's transition. The clear end and entrance into my season of Grace was evidenced by my having a benefit sold out concert to raise money for a trip to West Africa. Just like I couldn't escape the season of grief, this season of Grace is unfolding to become something that miracles are made of! Come on with me, let's continue as we grow from Grief to Grace.

Chapter 6

Death and Life, IS in What You Say

"Death and life are in the power of the tongue, and those who love it will eat its fruit."

— Proverbs 18:21 KJV

If there's any hope for humanity, we must all change the way we think and the way we speak. Another truism is, "Out of the abundance of the heart, the mouth speaks." Meaning the agreement will come out of your mouth revealing what you truly believe or think in your heart. From that confession will come the manifestation of those beliefs. I say if you really want to know what's with you, just listen to what comes out of your own mouth.

My beliefs have shaped my world! When I understood the knowledge that I am a Divine created being, a co-creator with God, I didn't want to accept, believe or be responsible for that fact. To say that my entire life, from the age of accountability, has been of my making is too heavy. I thought about all of the unfair and unwarranted situations that's happened to me. I thought about how I wasn't the kind of person that sat about thinking how I would misuse and abuse people. Taking advantage of their kindnesses or thinking of ways to prey upon them to deceive them. So, why was I getting all this mistreatment?

Again, I was only looking through the lens of the current *"season"* of suffering. Blinded by its pain and trauma, it totally eclipsed the *"seasons"* of blessings and prosperity and that world I had also created and the many lessons learned. In the bitterness of suffering, I failed to embrace all the positive things I had in fact accomplished and done well in my life. My conversation had changed. I no longer spoke of the beauty found in life as the chords of optimism vanished into thin air. If anyone around me began to speak of things good or positive, I would interject my bitterness and say things like, "yeah, but don't get too comfortable with it." or "you know it's only a matter of time before the real truth about it will be revealed." To say the least, cynicism, sarcasm had become the tone of the day for me. And in my mind, justifiably so. And worse still I was blind to it until someone that loved me gently spoke the truth to me. Of course I became immediately defensive, but because I knew the person was filled with no other motive but to see their sister walking light, and in the light again, I let down my defenses to receive what was being shared. I would like to interject at this point to say, people will say the most unhelpful, insensitive things during your grief and trauma. I highly encourage the reader to forgive them quickly. "It's their butts talking, because their mouths would have known better not to utter such." (side-eye, you can't see me giving.) No, but in all seriousness, just forgive them, because, unless they've been where you are, they don't know what to say. And if you need a Biblical, literature reference, read the book of Job and listen to what his friends say to this truly soul-traumatized man.

We live in a world of "conspiracies", not "conspiracy theories"; they're no longer theories when you can see the evidence of it. These are times when what we thought of as patriotic and true as the rising sun, are now being revealed to be lies and deceptions. We can see these in every institution known as pillars of our societal structures. From the economies of the world, to the religions of the world and everything in between, we are discovering many misnomers and blatant lies for things we hold as sacred truths. It's as if the whole world is awakening to the fact, like in the nursery rhyme, "Life is but a dream." We are discovering things long held and confessed as the gospel truths are anything but. This isn't cynicism speaking, this is awakening speaking.

When I began to listen to what was coming out of my mouth, I had to once again, get still. I have long known the truth of the saying, "if you listen long enough to someone, you'll learn what they really are about". Born with empathic abilities that give sensitivity to the emotions and energies about me, I can easily get over stimulated in my feelings. The "gift" is to be used for the overall ecosystem of humanity in what's understood as compassion; it's what makes us human. However, turned inward upon the self, it takes on an unhealthy state where emotions can become imbalanced by exaggerated highs and lows, demanding the need for balance and a healthy dose of reality. During that season of grief, I was vibrating on a very low frequency of negativity. "As a man thinks, so is he." I was thinking very low about myself and about life. Therefore, my conversations would be about the things I had lost and suffered. Since this was the manner of my conversation, the manifestations of lack, loss and emptiness in my life became reality. I was creating my world. A result of nature being created in the image and likeness of God.

Words are vibrationally powerful containers for death or for life. Back in the early 2000s a girlfriend of mine with whom I would gather weekly to pray, shared with me some information she'd come across about a book she'd been led to read by a Japanese businessman and author who published a book entitled "The Hidden Messages in Water" by Masaru Emoto. We were fascinated by his findings which only confirmed for us that the Bible was true in this matter of Proverbs 18:21. It proved to us what we were experiencing regarding this matter of our "conversations" and what we say indeed has a direct correlation to what experiences we can have. Mr. Emoto's published findings confirmed that we were not crazy and what we received in our times of prayer and meditations were real.

Now, mind you, I am in this "season" of grief, not connecting the dots between what's coming out of my mouth and what's manifesting in my life. Even though my girlfriend and I had, some seven years prior to the season, been given this huge revelation and understanding about the power of our words. It wasn't until I began to listen to what I was confessing when I opened my mouth that I truly understood the magnitude of my words. As optimistic and passionate as I had been about life and doing good in the world, I had become equally as dispassionate and hopeless about it. Nor was I fully understanding that I was creating my world of dispassion and hopelessness.

"Everything that can be shaken, will be shaken"

The world I knew, the America I thought I knew..., Everything was being shaken!

I began to listen to music about the injustices in the world and to watch documentaries and movies about real horrible accounts of racial injustices and social inequities and disparities. Living in my new community, I was faced daily with the reality of being Black in America. Contrary to popular belief, there are in fact "Two Americas", there's "White America" and then there's everyone else in America. This isn't a statement made out of cynicism, but reality. Our current headlines and social media are filled with videos and stories of brutalities and violence no matter the racial profile, but more prominent, those with "Black" America. In fact, we're just beginning to see the "Karens" of the world, the "Beckys" and "Biffs" in their native sense of entitlement wreaking havoc on society. So much so that even White Americans are ashamed of them, for them, and are speaking out against such behavior.

Things that have been going on for a long, long time but now made evident with the technology of smartphones and body cams, but even with all that a man can still be murdered before our very eyes by law enforcement by those sworn to protect and to serve. In one ruthless act, the trauma from slavery and all its ills rips off the delicate scab right from the minds of those indigenous descendants of the enslaved born in America, but never fully her citizen. Paralyzing the spectators of every ethnic group, they do nothing but scream like our ancestors while they watch the life of another human being viciously and violently snuffed out! A modern day lynching! A true psyop replayed and replayed across the media to remind a people traumatized at a cellular level of the code lodged in their DNA, disrupting the potential for healing and wholeness. My America, the land of "Brotherhood" did NOT include me or those who looked like me. More disappointment, despair and grief! And the whole world saw it and was enraged!

Once Again, I was ruefully awakened to reality, to my real reality as an "American Citizen" born and bred, yet still in a caste where the "right" to vote even to this day has to be voted upon and passed by an act of Congress! You mean to tell me that an immigrant born on another soil, especially if they're of European descent, can come here and be afforded great privileges and opportunities by becoming a citizen through an oath and will never have to worry about having a right to vote, among other things? Yet me, a naturalized born "American", and those of my lineage do? What the hell?!!! Sooo, after four hundred plus years, when will we ever BE citizens?

That's what I wanted to know, because I was in this weird space of having known some of the luxury of suburban living and culture to now living, yet again at the poverty level statistically fitting all of the markers of being in a caste system in the wealthiest nation on earth. Here I am, living a lifestyle of poverty, none of which I thought at the time was my choice. When I was a child, and we were poor, I didn't know I was poor! All of "Black America" was poor and in the struggle. They programmed us that it was "good times" and we sang it with a smile. How the hell did I get here?!!! I mean, wasn't I just flying first class and seeing beautiful Puerto Rico and Belize?!!! Like, didn't I just go to Hawaii and see where they filmed "Pirates of the Caribbean"?!!! Hadn't I just been flown in to perform for a major north american convention?!!! "What is REALLY going on?" was the question in my mind and mouth. I was no longer in a dream, like the nursery rhyme. Somewhere along my journey, I obviously took the "red pill"! I was AWAKE! I was aware and the reality was too much! Depression was a new companion whose company I despised.

As a people, we've always known that the rules and standards were different. Hollywood and independent filmmakers, authors and songwriters alike have produced enough bodies of works to remind us of the countless stories and accounts of heinous mistreatment, terroristic acts and injustices against the descendants of the enslaved in this nation. I was in a collective type of pain. I realized that I too had believed the delusion that I was separate, but equal. It's the conversations we have as families and confidants when we're not "code-shifting" to get along in "White-America". Isn't that what history books really taught, we're separate, but more like unequal? In Christianity, I was a "suffering saint" as it says, "...all who desire to live godly shall suffer persecution." 2 Tim. 3:12. I was indoctrinated to wait to get my reward on the other side, in the sweet by and by! We even sang songs about it. The truth is, just like the home environment I was raised in was dysfunctional, it was in fact the microcosm of the American macrocosm. Mother America is psychotic. She hasn't dealt with her issues and her choices to do harm and cause injury, so her children continue to pay the price. Remember how I said earlier that the psychological health of the mother is key to having a womb healthy enough to carry, support and sustain life psychologically and physically.

I was now a mother who experientially understood the deep heart-breaking pain of the death of a child, even though an adult child. I now felt akin to every mother that has, or ever would lose their child due to some act of violence, disease or accident. Like, why was all this pain and grief so new, yet so familiar to me? I had not suffered the violence of racism to the same degree as countless others. I was now living with not only my grief, but a collective grief. There were those like so many in the news media outlets, that I cannot mention by name in this book, due to legalities, but I say their names and I pray for their parents because I know what that kind of trauma feels like. I feel for parents in war torn countries caught in the crossfire and those whose children have been snatched away as a result of being kidnapped or just missing and never found.

In spite of all that, I began identifying with all that was wrong in belonging to a particular people group in America with a unique heritage and history. The evangelical world was turned upside down on its head, when former President Barack Husain Obama ran for the highest office in the land. Although none of us knew who he was, this democrat from Illinois, he was taking the nation and the world by storm. "Obama Fever" was everywhere! For most Black Americans it was the long-awaited "Change" so many had given their lives for and their allegiance to. The fervor and fever-pitched political scene proved to be like a rash outbreak in White America! In 2008, I was in Israel during the time of his candidacy before his first term.

Remember what I said about listening to people long enough, you'll discover what they're really about. Well, I will suffice to say, the woman that served as my host while there, an "Eskenazi Jewish woman" I had met the year before when I was there, showed out! I mean she couldn't hide her disdain for Mr. Obama, and her prejudices. So ironic that here she was hosting a black woman in her home under the auspice of "Christian love and brotherhood" accusing the man of ill intent before he even won the election, while excusing and wanting prayers for the current sitting president, with known transgressions against innocent peoples while under his watch. It was unbelievable. I was so disappointed. It was a crazy time and people who once "broke bread" together and held prayer meetings and bible studies together soon found themselves careening down a mountain of dung with all of its putridness revealing a great divide. It was also the year I realized I wasn't just living in "Two Americas" I had been living in what became to be revealed as the "Twins of Christianity". For many "white" and "black" "Christians" alike, the "Love" had not covered a multitude of sins. That was also the year I decided I'd had enough of being christianized, politicized and mesmerized, I was awakened and had met the real god in evangelicalism... "Politics".

It's 2016 and I'm living in a haze of "Are you kidding me right now?!" I'm meeting and bonding with new people, discovering new information from Black Historians and Social Keepers of Black Consciousness. I'm on this huge learning curve of who I am now in this "new, but not new reality". I'm being introduced to myself daily. My words are laced with bitterness and sarcasm as I dialog with people of like pain, trauma and disappointment. I began to move away from the circles of my evangelical associations because of the painful reality of divided hearts about the prejudices based on the color of a man's skin, a man who looked like me and my people, and not the content of his character! I had been born into this world, into this nation in 1964 with all the same trauma and drama still alive and well, these many years later. One day I heard my mouth say... "What the hell have we been doing these last fifty-plus years?!!" I had had enough! During that time, I wasn't thinking that this "black-skinned" Mulatto was in any way different than his predecessors, but the Obama Craze was on in the African-American communities across the nation. I could find the excitement that so many were feeling. I knew that I sensed another disappointment was on the way. We as a people hadn't learned the lesson that no one person was coming to save us. We would fail the test again. Now in hindsight, I was vindicated. My private thoughts, intuition hadn't lied to me.

Boy, my mouth had gotten as "salty" as my personality that had taken on a completely new identity. This "new" Evelyn was losing the focus of her light. I found that I was attracting like energy from people, like myself, clearly awakened to the harsh realities of life and living in America. The bitterness and the grief in my heart was finding its life through the dark and disappointing realities of fallen humanity. I talked about the systemic economic injustices of us American descendants of the enslaved . I read books and published articles about *Food Deserts* and Jim Crow, yet alive in another form. Books that addressed the truths about systemic racism and systemic economic inequities. Elders, Ancestors and contemporaries are enlightening me to knowledge, history and science that was never expressed in my evangelical circles of association (Black or White) nor of my formal educational process. But I'd found group, after group and a soapbox to espouse my new ideologies, knowledge and understanding on. My words spoke of all the negative issues we continue to blatantly face. What had been just under the surface on this American soil had begun to boil. It was like my very life was being played out in synchronicity in the current events of the times!!!

My new group of associates were fascinating! Some of the most intelligent young adults of all ethnicities, religions and racial groups, who gave me hope for future generations. Unrealized at the time, but now evident in hindsight, these new groups I began to form relationships with had a common experience and a common undercurrent, the pain of *trauma*! We are the descendants of traumatized people who have yet to be restored. And the descendants of those who perpetrated the trauma and the privileges it afforded them were equally traumatized by the truth. It was all because, *Trauma is trauma, is trauma!*

Joshua's "**death**" had brought forth a new reality in me. The vocabulary of my daily discourses had taken on such negativity and sharpness. In the "biblical" sense, I had become like one of the characters written therein. In the book of Ruth, there's the account of a woman named Naomi, a respectable family within their community. At the leading of her husband, she and her entire family went to a distant land full and prosperous, to escape the famine in their home country. In the process of time while in the foreign land, her husband and her two sons die and she's left alone with her two daughter-in-laws, all three of them now widows (a serious economic devastation). One of the daughters decides to return to her people after the urging of her mother-in-law rather than suffer the dismal looking future with her, while Ruth decides she will remain. Talking about being able to identify with this woman's bitterness! I would even say sarcastically to my sistah-girl, "Don't call me Evelyn, call me Mara! Chile' I'm just like Naomi in the bible!" Although I'd say it with a voice of humor, I was so serious.

For years I'd been running from the bitterness I'd seen in my mother as a result of her own grieving. During the years following the marriage to my first husband, I had prayed to overcome being bitter and up until now, I had won the fight. However, this was a new fight, and I'm the only one in the ring and I was losing ground. As Divine Spirit would have it, the revelation came, and I got it! I understood my mother and myself like never before. I was drinking from the fountain of bitterness, sharing my cup and the cups of others, dead or alive. All my thoughts were on life's injustices and woeful inequities. I was becoming a champion of social injustices and an "in your face" social media influencer to expose the "culture vultures" in society, especially those within my community and sphere of influence.

I began to get involved with organizations committed to "bringing lasting change" denied by all the politicians and presidents of this nation, past and currently sitting. As passionate as I was about sharing the Evangelical's version of the "Good News", I was fast becoming just as passionate about sharing and imparting the truths of history and information long suppressed and ignored by mainstream western media and historians. Wasn't I right to feel this way? We've all been lied to! After all, the truth of the matter is life **IS** bitter. My mouth was becoming a fountain of bitter water, so to speak.

You see, I had begun to bond with trauma once again in its various forms. Why? Because I was born into it. I knew its familiar energy at a cellular level. In my new circles, we bonded over the traumas of being Black in America and the collective experiences found in our generations. It was the stench of decay, the dying of a particular group of people and it seems no one serving in the seat of power cares. It was pain, it was grief, it was trauma so I was in there. Committed like a magnet to metal. Even though I failed again to recognize it for what it was, I was bonded to it. It had a cause and I would be its champion because I have lived it!

As I began to become more familiar with certain groups and organizations. However, I began to see a certain pattern in them all. There was this undercurrent of hostile internal discourse within the inner circles of every group I began to associate with. No matter how noble the work and vision, I sensed something is obviously deeply out of alignment within the psyche of "Black" people, my people, me. *The ability to find a harmonious congruence within that flows outward creating a oneness.* I noticed that there were key words (trigger words) that could often be found in the writings and dialogues of these groups. Words like "disadvantaged", "at-risk", "victims of society" "minorities" and "marginalized", "under-served", "displaced" etc. But I digress, this book isn't about my ever evolving religious or political views or the constructs held to measure my life within the society I find myself, but rather about how my thoughts and words dictate in the way I choose to show up in the midst of society. How I arrived at embracing the season of grief to the newness of life.

In my own vocabulary, I was using words like "broken-hearted", "disappointed", "Death", "loss", "grief", and "despair". Before I go further, I want to say that these words have their place, however, what I am about to emphasize is the **power** of identifying **with** or being identified **by** them.

Without going too deep here, I want to touch on the words *"death", "Loss" "Void"* and *"Transition".* By etymology, the word ***death*** originated as, (Old English deaþ noun, "total cessation of life, act or fact of dying, state of being dead;); ***Loss*** is originated as, Old English los "ruin, destruction," from Proto-Germanic *lausa- (from PIE root *leu- "to loosen, divide, cut apart"); ***Transition*** is originated as, mid-15c., transicion, in grammar, from Latin "transitionem" (nominative transitio) "a going across or over," noun of action from past-participle stem of transire "go or cross over". Which leads us to the adjective meaning, **transient** (adj.) c. 1600, "transitory, not durable," from Latin "transientem" (nominative transiens) "passing over or away," present participle of transire "cross over, go over, pass over, hasten over, pass away," from trans "across, beyond" (see trans-) + ire "to go" (from PIE root *ei- "to go"). Meaning "passing through a place without staying" is from the 1680s. Sourced from Etymonline.com. ***void*** *(n.)*

1610s, "unfilled space, gap," from void (adj.). Meaning "absolute empty space, vacuum" is from 1727. Etymonline.com

In the English language, the word death in its truest meaning has with it a clear connotation of something/someone being without life. Loss in its truest meaning has with it a clear connotation of something/someone being destroyed or apart from. ***Transition*** in its truest meaning has with it a clear connotation of something/someone having crossed over, passed over, or passing through. Void in its truest meaning has with it a clear connotation of an "unfilled space, gap," an "absolute empty space, vacuum."

To say that something or someone is **dead** or has **died** is accurate in the sense that what was an aspect about the person or thing no longer exists is true. To say of Loss in the same context is true in that the person or thing is no longer physically with you, but it's not destroyed.

Understanding the power of words and their ability to contain or hold many kinds of emotions, I found a sense of well-being developing when I was made self-aware of my expressions and emotions when using certain words.

Words like *transition* and *void* held a certain vibration of positivity which gave me a greater sense of comfort. What I mean is this, we should all understand that with sound there's certain vibrations that can evoke a particular reaction. Think of it like this, when you're watching a movie, say a scene is depicted as scary or wants to invoke fear, the soundtrack plays dissonant and minor chords. If there's dialogue, certain words are used to underscore the evil intent or harm. Even though the body is sitting in the comfort and safety of the home or theater, the brain reacts with the same energy of fight/flight as if the situation was real! The brain cannot differentiate whether the event is happening literally or not. The blood's chemistry is all the same whether real or imagined.

The intense feelings are happening just by what's being heard. Try watching the same scene that's getting intense with a violence and mute the sound; you'll discover a decrease in anxiety within the body. Although visually you are stimulated because of what the eyes are taking in, the experience isn't as stimulating to the senses without sound. Have you ever wondered what in today's movies we constantly hear the "F-bomb" being dropped? I mean, it's like the manuscript must meet a quota of 'F-bombs" to even make the grade! Maybe it's just me, but it's that thing that makes me go... humm?

In the Bible, Christ is recorded as having said, "...the words that I speak unto you, they are spirit, and they are life." (John 6:63) This is implied to mean that the very things spoken affect the spirit and can bring forth life from the psyche or soul. Conversely, words spoken can bring death. My point in this is, depending on the words you use, i.e. speak, will depend on whether your experiences with the season of grief will bring forth life or death in you. How's that for being responsible to yourself?

In truth, I was creating my world and all that was around me by the words I was using. By the statements being made. By the conversations I was indulging in. By the messages I was listening to. My ear and eye gates were being saturated with negative visions and sounds. I found solace in the pain and shared traumas of others. Ironically, before my experience with Joshua's **transition**, I hadn't been as intimately acquainted with so much grief and sorrow. During the season of grief, I found more and more associations, situations and issues of trauma and loss to identify with and was drawn to. It seemed that I became the poster child for every injustice and grief known to man. I even found "solace" in the Bible where it says in the book of Isaiah speaking prophetically of the Christ, "...He was a man of sorrows, acquainted with grief..." Well, just put my name right there in the middle of that scripture with the good Lord Jesus, because I was definitely that! Now, even the bible was cosigning on my pain. I was justified, right? NOT!

What I was, was accountable! I was now held accountable for the truths I had come to know and understand about the power and meaning of these words, of all words and the conversations and narratives I will speak within. "Out of the abundance of the heart, the mouth speaks." (Matt. 12:34) It was like, all the years over my lifetime came flooding down on me like a waterfall! Having been a student of the Word of God at a very young age; facilitating prayer groups, study groups and small groups; admonishing the lifestyle of faithfulness to the scriptures and the principles therein with the many speaking engagements and conferences; the trainings in counseling, in biblical "self-confrontation"; the disciplines of self-awareness and personal devotion to morals and principles; this was my pedigree. And now, a deluge of revelation and understanding about choosing life over death, peace over pain, purpose over perception, I was being swept downstream in rapid rivers, struggling to swim and trying not to drown.

There was no denying that the pain was real and that I felt what I felt. Everyone feels what they feel. However, now it was about what I would *DO* with it all?!!! In all of my well-intentioned self to be a "godly" "Christian" (i.e. child of God, a "moral" wife, mother, daughter, sister, and friend) none of that had shielded me from the traumas my soul experienced. From my formative years with a parent clearly suffering from grief and depression to my present dilemmas wrestling with grief and racism alive and well in all its realities. No, such devotion had shielded me from the pain and disappointments of the divorce(s) or the death of my personal dreams, aspirations, expectations and imaginations I'd held for myself. None of it shielded me or my sons or the sons of my friends who had "African-American" sons from having to give them the talk about "surviving the encounter". It was all grievous! And Joshua's **death** seemed the catalyst to bring it all to the surface. Nothing shielded me from my not understanding and feeling disappointed even by God.

My life was staring me blatantly in my face demanding that I make a decision about what I was going to do with this grief "new normal!!!" My God, how I hated that term! Even though I know it was/is the most apropos use of such a term, I didn't want any of what I was going through to become anywhere near a sense of being "normal"! Someone has said that "normal" is just a setting on the dryer! Lol! Like, what's "normal" really??? The longer you live, you find out just how jacked up we ALL are! Everyone, and I do mean EVERYONE has issues! The only people that don't are under them about six feet.

In 2017, thanks to my big Sister, I took a trip to San Diego, California to attend a speaker's and writer's conference being held by an internationally known best-selling author and motivator. This woman's story resonated with me and her persona was much like my own. During that conference attended by well above fifteen hundred people, pre-covid, I was still accompanied by Grief & Grace, trying to find some sense of purpose in life. I knew I wanted to be a writer and I was already a professional speaker and singer. So, I took a leap and went. I literally thought, what the hell, if I keep waking up everyday, I better find some kind of redemptive measure for all this pain. Smh! Terrible I know!

While there in the conference, when I shared about wanting to write about the seasons of life and grief and the very real human experiences accompanied with it, well my circle in the setting became that much smaller. There were people there from all over the United States and several other countries with their aspirations of writing the next number one best seller or having a top-rated podcast or speaking circuit about the positive side of life. About achieving goals and dreams and becoming your best you! Not death, as though taboo, when everyone without exception must make its acquaintance. I mean it almost became laughable! I was undoubtedly the "Debbie Downer" in the group, in the conference. I mean people in my breakout group sessions just didn't want to deal with such a heavy subject matter. It was like some of their facial expressions said, "I didn't come all this way this weekend to deal with this woman's pain and grief! But being the Empath that I am, I sensed a lot of grief in that conference. There were smiling faces hiding behind the grief and pain of dead entrepreneurial ventures, dead business, dead family units and relationships. All being the fodder for why they'd come to develop a skill set in communication. I mean so many had those "death" tales of loss and overcoming the sense of failure when things went south. It was so ironic to me that none could see that had those situations not died, they probably wouldn't even be at the conference.

I found only one other person attending the conference that understood the need for such writings and she'd actually published her book and was a vendor there. Of course we connected and discussed the need for such books and courses. The conference was a lifeline of hope in the midst of a raging sea of uncertainty. But another unlikely encounter while there came during a one on one session with one of the volunteers vetted to conduct a mini-coaching session with attendees who signed up for them. I don't remember the lady's name, but her spirit was pure. After hearing my "elevator speech" replete with all my language of grief, death and loss, all I remember her saying is, "Evelyn, you're trying not to feel the pain of your son's death. But you're always going to feel it. The answer you want is, how are you going to *live* with it? In that brief twenty-five minute coaching session, she saw me clearly and I hadn't even divulged one third of my story.

The season of grief was served to me on a silver platter in order for me to learn and to understand the ecosystem that I've been born into, meaning the world around me. We say all the time, "we've brought nothing into this world and we'll take nothing out." "You don't see a moving truck behind a hearse." Clearly, everything we have in this "life" experience is temporary and for this life experience, yet we focus on the temporal as though it is eternal. As I stated, I was born in 1964 and although I have lived long enough to know a few things, not **believe** but to **know**, by experience and intimate acquaintance, not much has changed. Which has given me my life's motto:

My intimacy with grief has brought about a phenomenal life exchange. I have truly evolved into someone I'm getting to know. It's now a beautiful awakening of daily discovery, to relearn me in relation to the world around me with this **void** I now carry within my heart. As a Human being I have the ability to create my world of understanding through the perceptions and usage of Divine Nature, using the tools of spirit-led reasoning within the ecosystem we call life. Having a divine connection to all that is, as an energetic being within a vast universe, my embracing of the grief season brought forth life, once I changed my language (words) to express it. Once I changed my perceptions about it. Once I stopped resisting it.

The power of pain reveals so much to us about us, our bodies, and our relationships. Many have taken the bitter fruit of pain and have allowed it to nourish and to supply the psyche with manifold expressions of peace and hope. Conversely, many have taken it with bitterness and have become as bitter as the pain itself. They haven't come to embrace the season for what it is/was, and the fruit therein as an overall part of their human experience. But rather, they become stuck in the *season* redefining their overall life experience by the one scene or scenes in their life. Imagine watching an entire theatrical production and forgetting all the many beautiful scenes and dialogues because in act five, scene ten your hero or heroine was unexpectedly murdered, killed off or died! Your hopes, dreams and expectations are destroyed. The ending you'd imagined was now dashed and you're faced with an unexpected outcome.

You come out of the theater mournful and bewildered not understanding *why* your favorite character(s) were killed off! You totally disregard acts one through four and all of the beautiful scenes therein, your focus becomes that one scene where your hero/heroine dies and your dreams fade to black. You begin to recount the story to others when they ask you about the play, you begin at the death, at the loss, at the grief, not at the life and all that was beneficial as a result of what made the character special or endeared to you. You rehearse the disappointment, hurt and the trauma. You think about the scene(s) and replay them repeatedly in your mind until it becomes the thing you wake up with and go to bed with. You retell it over and over until anything positive or beautiful is lost in the translation of your negative narrative in the experience. It becomes your story and you tell it with pride. Yes, pride!

Worse still, are those who never even speak of the "play" ever again, NEVER! Their hero/heroine is suddenly, traumatically taken off the scene and in the shock and dismay of it, the person never "speaks" of it again. They won't allow others around them to speak of it. In fact, to make any mention of the matter will constitute what they would consider, "justifiable rage" or "solicited mistreatment" from them. Those closest to these individuals will have to learn how to tip-toe among the mines in the minefields of their psyche so as not to trigger them and incur their wrath whether verbal or physical.

Then, perhaps there are those who, being traumatized, become one of the "living dead", a zombie to life. A person walking in life by anesthetizing their pain through substance abuse wanting an escape from the experience of trauma to the soul. Sadly inflicting more pain upon themselves by overeating, substance abuse, cutting or excessive mistreatment of the body through masochism. Often such individuals find themselves repeatedly in unhealthy relationships where abuse will be inevitable. You get my point with the analogy, yes?

"Be the Light you want to see, the Joy you want to feel, the Love you want to know".

My Lesson

I will say, we truly do create our world by the way we think and the power of our words. There's a verse that says men will give an account for every "idle" word spoken. Now whether you believe in a day when all that is will stand before a supreme judge or not, that's your free will. But the weight of words must be profound if men will be held accountable for EVERY IDLE WORD! Means words that we use without purpose or effect. A pointless word(s), empty chatter. "Why?" is the question we should be asking ourselves. Why will men be held accountable for speaking idly? I am convinced that it's because it's our greatest "Godlike" attribute! Being products of the Divine Nature, created in the image and likeness of the All Supreme Universal Most High. It is said that all things consist and are held together by the power of Infinite Word. It would stand to reason then that we too have the capacity to create by the things we imagine and speak. There was a time when a man's word was his bond. What happened to that? We all know how we feel when people don't keep their word, even when we don't keep our word. Words are powerful! The deadliest childhood rhyme and lie ever repeated was, "Sticks and stones may break my bones, but words will never harm me." Words not only harm, but they kill, steal and destroy!

If our world teaches us anything, it teaches us there is a universal law at work in our system. Put whatever label you want to put on it, "resopricity", "give and take", "yin/yang", "what goes around, comes around", "karma", "reaping and sowing", "As a man thinks" "To do is to be" whatever! The point is, we as human beings have attempted to verbalize and characterize these universal truths in every culture and civilization. Making the correlation between the spoken word, what is said and the manifested word, what that word creates! That you will get back what you put out. Because before we do ANYTHING we have a conversation about it. Whether without or within, words are given as the energy to thoughts.

A declaration, an edict, a proclamation goes forth, then it is followed by an execution of the words therein. We know that we are Divine BEings with the ability to create because we have the ability to speak. It's just that simple! Speech and reason is what separates us from the other kinds/kingdoms of species within this system. All that we see and experience in the material world is the evidence of someone's speech made manifest from their imagination whether written or verbalized. The words contained either offer life or death.

We should all know by now, that if a child in the formative years is spoken to with harshness or constant belittlement and suffers demonstrations of ill-treatment, that spirit will be greatly damaged and its growth most likely stunted. However, conversely if spoken to with words and demonstrations of positivity and empowerment, that spirit has a fighting chance to develop for the overall good of humanity. What do we mean when we hear sociologists speak of healing the inner child? What does it mean in our societies when we find publications on "How to's"? Because we ultimately know something is off, something isn't quite right or is out of alignment.

We should be asking ourselves, "when did we become so negative?" What made me feel so helpless and powerless. What has happened to me, that I feel like an imposter to my own life? Now unless a person is afflicted with a personality disorder or malady, like narcissistic personality disorder, having the inability to show or experience empathy, we can all know when we are out of harmony or balance with ourselves or others. Even at times when we ignore our own intuitions, for the sake of being nice, we ultimately experience regret because we did.

I clearly created my world of grief and dysfunction. I was the cause of the major changes in my lifestyle and in my aspirations. I determined through a series of perceptions and thoughts to define my life by one experience and not by the overall journey up to that point. In that space and time I felt the entire weight of my choices and words. The death I had come to know and the grief associated with it had manifested in my life. Because I had said this life was meaningless, and had lost its meaning. Because I had said that it was pointless to try and pursue anything, anymore, dreams and aspirations dissipated from my life. These things I spoke audibly and subconsciously. Remember my earlier reference about the scientific discovery of the impact words have on water? Well, if the human adult body is made of up to 60 percent water, can you imagine what my words were doing to my cells? Trust me it manifested in my beautiful locs going from being healthy, shining and full to shriveling up and breaking off. My once youthful, glowing skin began to exhibit a darkened scaliness and dryness. My cuticles and nails became very dry and brittle. My joints began to ache and I began to have symptoms of arthritis and tendonitis. When you're dry within, like a parched desert, you lose your craving for water, even. I lost my thirst and I was falling apart.

I basically became a slave to my pain and my grief. I gave my power over to the mundane and to the routines of life that didn't require any inspiration or aspiration. I came to understand how people become addicts and complacent to the point of giving up. I was filled with the revelation that in as much as I had been given the fortune and opportunity to know some of the most fulfilling experiences a human can have, I also came to understand the depths to which a person can sink if their thoughts and words are out of alignment with their Divine Nature.

I had to take responsibility and be accountable to myself. To be committed to myself in honor of the Divine Nature within me to *CHANGE!* We humans really do not like change, especially when it requires a sacrifice. When I began to change my conversation and my choice of words to things in keeping with gratitude, thanksgiving and positivity, I began recreating a new reality for myself, post trauma. Death and Life is truly in what you say.

Chapter 7

Abundance, Alignment, All Is Well!

Abundance After Coming Through the Storm

The season of grief was a long and tedious one. The lessons learned therein invaluable, reaping a harvest of gratitude that I am and will forever be thankful for.

I have lived long enough to know that death is really about living. I mean, you really don't start living until you die. The death of the self, begins the resurrected life, the life you and I were truly meant to live. In dying to the false narratives and expectations we hold to be sacred to us, we become free. In our station in life, whether rich or poor, when we detach from it all, the perceptions and our imaginations of our sense of worth, we then discover our real value or worth, which is more than anything this material world holds. This is when you find the "I Am" within.

Beginning each new day with a blank canvas unafraid to face it with all the possible energies of positivity and abundance. Even in the face of negativity which appears to only accentuate the positive, I embrace it now not as opposition, but rather as an opportunity that excites me to awaken and greet the day.

A shift of mindset and perception is the key to healing oneself. It is taking the power to shift your mood. Taking those things that serve us in becoming our highest self and the best version of who we are made to be is always in order. I remember in the days of my small group classes that I facilitated saying, "you don't see a tree struggling to be trees' or rocks reeling to be rocks' or dogs and cats deliberating and conversing on how to be canines and felines, but yet we struggle and debate on what it is and means to be Human BEings. The following excerpt is from a post I made on my "Grief2Grace" Facebook Social Media page, which came to me in the year 2017. The funny thing is, I wasn't even where I am now in knowledge and understanding, but the writing was like a prophecy to myself.

> *The beautiful side of grief! A short three years ago... you could have NEVER told me that I would see beauty in the season of grief! Most don't grieve holistically realizing that loss is the same side of the coin as gain. As death is to life, so is profit to loss; positive to negative, yin to yang! Experiencing the fullness of any season, the season of grief in particular, the "death" of someone or something is just a marker for time. When we understand we're eternal beings having a human experience; we'll know with understanding that it is the pain of death that lets you know you're alive!!! It too is a passing season that lets you know you have truly lived, loved, & labored. So don't get stuck! BE your authentic self! #grief2grace*

Wow! I've had to go back to reread that post and even tweak a bit grammatically because I knew what I was trying to express. Even then, at the time of its posting, all was not fully actualized yet, the seeds or the buddings of wisdom, growth, and understanding with change were there. Having an abundance of knowledge will only lead to poverty of spirit if it is not applied with wisdom and discipline. Just like a person can have an abundance of money, but if not utilized properly, they will soon be poor again. What's the old adage? "A fool and his money will soon depart." It's true, we will soon lose the person and things that come to bring us life abundantly if we mishandle and abuse them because we fail to understand their purpose in our lives for the season.

It will be well warranted to pay attention and to focus on the positive things in life especially during a season of grief or loss. The truth is whatever was gained before can be gained again. To have a poverty spirit or mindset will only produce more of the same. Then there is that... "Blessed are the poor in spirit, for theirs is the Kingdom of Heaven." Matt. 5:3, KJV. This truism isn't for the "sweet by and by" but needfully for the here and now. When we begin to actually apply the principles of these sacred writing to our lives, we'll find our perspectives will change and so will our circumstances. Abundance comes, not through the amassment of material things or accomplishments, but the true abundance of the soul comes through the understanding of one's self in relation to such things. We are not to be a slave to *things*, but rather the *things* serve us. Just as when we come to understand that all of life is one big classroom with many lessons to be learned in becoming as (KRST) or Christ as is more familiar to most. How do we know this is true? Because like I said before, every material thing we possess is for this life we take none of it with us when we make our transition. Our titles and legacy are only as relevant as those who hold us in remembrance. Think of the billions of people we have or will never know of, yet during their time on earth they meant something to someone. They accomplished some mighty works for the sake of those they love and for humanity. I'm past certain it's because they too found the keys to life in this realm.

They understood it's the sacrifice of the ego, the dying to self in order to really experience living. This IS The Abundant Life of Christ (KRST).

Alignment with Agreement (Getting Back to Center)

Once I returned to my center in the Divine Nature of who I was made to be and to the work I was called to do, I found the Alignment needed to prosper once again. Remember the dream I mentioned at the beginning of the book? Please read below...

One night I had a nightmare, a dream vivid and in full color. In the dream, I was out walking with Joshua, who could have only been about two or three years old in the dream, (but was an infant sleeping in his bassinet at the foot of our bed in reality). There we were, holding hands walking down a neighborhood street filled with manicured lawns on a glorious sunny day. A day bright with warmth, fresh air and sunshine, but it was not our neighborhood. As we walked along, I noticed that I was not walking alongside the row of cars, being careful to have my son closer to the lawns on the sidewalk, but rather he was on the outside as it were, walking closest to the cars. Then suddenly, in a moment like a split second, Joshua snatched away from my hand and ran between the cars into the street! I heard the impact, and the screeching of the tires, but I didn't see the impact. In the dream I screamed a wailing from my soul that was only heard in reality the day I received the phone call of his death—- and that moment in the shower.

I awaked from the dream hysterical, and I frantically jumped out of bed over to our son's bassinet only to find him peacefully sleeping. His father, startled from sleep, thrusted into my moment of hysteria, was processing his fight or flight responses as he tried to figure out the reasons for my wailing and tears. "Girl, what's wrong? He yelled excitedly, "Is something wrong with the baby???!" I could barely speak, because the images from the nightmare were at the forefront in my mind. The sound of the screeching tires, the impact, I was beside myself. I was so real. Calming down as I realized it had in fact been a dream, I was so shaken physically, that all my then-husband could do was hold me to console me. I eventually told him of the nightmare and we quietly prayed for it's meaning. For years as Joshua grew, the dream was always in the back of my mind and you better believe we never walked down a neighborhood street without him securely tethered to me. Over the years, I surmised many meanings of the dream, but the true meaning of it was actualized in the shower the morning I would be burying my firstborn son. So, I had in fact been told, shown ahead of time. In the spirit of me (My Divine Nature) it had been revealed. And as with so many of my other "peculiar instances" in my life, this experience fits the bill of Divine revelation. My tears in the shower that morning ceased and I knew I wasn't alone in this experience, my Father/Mother was with me and I would be given the strength necessary to get through the days ahead. End of dream.

That day and in that moment I knew that my life's journey had already been written. I discovered in the subsequent days following Joshua's transition, many more revelations and understandings he came to teach me and is still teaching me. His zeal and zest for life convinces me that as his memorial bookmark so aptly describes, he didn't come to stay. My ultimate agreement with The Creator's will for this precious soul as well as for my own has taken the "sting" out of death and destroyed the fear of it because the soul never dies! Whew!

For all the craziness before, during and after Joshua's transition I will always benefit from the lessons and the experiences. I don't bear shame as I know my choices were for the greater gain..., to learn the lessons in becoming (KRST) Christ-like in nature. Death in all of its forms produces life when we understand that just like the figure "8" eight, it's all reciprocal apart of the eternal order. My marriages that ended in divorce were not "failures" but rather "lessons learned" passing through those seasons as joyful and as difficult as they were, taught me, it didn't kill me. And there's another old adage, "Whatever doesn't kill you makes you stronger." It's true!

Aligning with Truth by revelation, and the understanding of it for you, is the highest form of God-consciousness there is. No two of His/Her children are the same and it takes a mighty One such as The Creator to manage all the "uniqueness" on this planet for all these millennia. Aligning with the Love energy, as said by the one called "The Apostle Paul" in the biblical literature "Brethren, I count not myself to have apprehended: but this one thing I do, forgetting those things which are behind, and reaching forth unto those things which are before, I press toward the mark for the prize of the high calling of God in (KRST) Christ Jesus. Phil. 3:13-14.

The living esoteric meaning of this is... not that we will ever attain perfection in this life journey, but we must deal with the seat of our emotions, our memories and how they will impact us. In order to forget, implies we must have something to remember. Notice where the forgetting lies... *behind us.*

Some people say I will never forget this or that, and we can see the reality of it, they have never progressed beyond that point in their lives either. Not a judgment, but an observation. Even the successful things in life, we must leave behind. Notice he didn't say, forgetting those bad or good things which are behind, he said things as all encompassing. My youngest son still struggles with his brother's death among many other issues from the choices in his life.

One day as I was being patient with him, understanding the sense of void he feels, I listened to all his rantings and sense of victimization and the myriad of unhealthy relationships he's **passed** through. I now was in a better place of mental health, spiritual growth and understanding that I could no longer co-sign on his perceptions of things. So I said, "son, we need to take a trip and go to each of these destinations where each of these situations are. So, I'm going to need you to give me a list of all these people and the places so we can confront the matter and them and be done with it once and for all.

Now, this might take a while with people's schedules being what they are, but we need to do this for you. You must settle this so you can move forward. So, where are we going first and who will we be seeing? As you can imagine, there was silence, because in that moment he realized that all of everything and everyone was in the past. It didn't matter if it was two days or twenty years in the past, **it was in the past**. I do understand my son, I have empathy for his pain. However, I do know that he rehearses the hurt and that he's more addicted to pain and trauma than he is to health and wholeness in this season in his life.

But above all that I was standing before him as a living witness that when I aligned myself with my truth and did the hard work of "Shadow Work" I understood like never before, my son won't be healed until he does that same hard work! Self-Confrontation. Loving yourself enough to deal with you, the real you. I would venture to say reader, and neither will you. In another season of my life I used to sell make-up, fragrance and nail products for a nationally known cosmetic company. There was a mantra I learned in that group which said, "Until the pain of the same becomes greater than the pain of change, people won't change."

With the heart-sigh that only a mother can sigh, I mentally released my son that day. Respecting The Creator's order of divinity within every soul. I know there's nothing I can do to change or my son's path for it is his path and he will make it what he wills. I no longer live with anxiety or guilt regarding his life because as an imperfect parent, I gave birth to imperfect children, I am of an imperfect species. I do pray for my son and when his mind is open to receive, I can sometimes give him words of wisdom and encouragement.

My son is like me in many ways. He has overcome many trials and if you think I can sing, boy, you haven't heard him! I admire his tenacity, however, there's much work ahead of him to find the peace, harmony and balance I'm writing about in this book. When he reads what I have written, I want him and you to know that I am above all others his greatest cheerleader. However, when it comes to bearing the responsibility of governing the spirit we all will give an account for ourselves and there's nothing we in and of ourselves can do to change that for another soul no matter how much we love them.

My Lesson

All is well. It shall be well.

"I did not incarnate in this life to stay. For there are many, many lessons to learn along the way. The path I'm on was chosen for me, I was given the power of choice to decide my destiny. The words I speak will condemn or bless. They will make my life a joy or a begrudging mess. I cannot blame another soul, if I should live beneath The Creator's goal. To live is (KRST) Christ and to die is gain, to overcome life's "opportunities" is the name of the game!

I have but one mission in life to attain, that I live up to my Creator's Name... I AM.

In that image, I AM love; I AM powerful; I AM successful; I AM prosperous; I AM joy, peace, patience, righteousness, forgiven, accountable, loyal, devoted, healthy, whole, compassionate,

I AM who I was made to be and the half hasn't been told.

I AM a Human BEing, "BOUNDLESS ENERGY" and I am at PEACE!"

Conclusion

Paralyzed by the perceptions of who we perceive ourselves to be. Statement: "I am worth the work! Do the work! It will be worth it!"

We are Spirit beings having a human experience. We are forms of energy and light encased in an avatar which allows us connection with matter. We have been evolving for millenia and will continue to. The usage of such terminology, aptly expresses with language things long experienced, but now I can communicate. As I said, as a child, I was often called an "old soul". This description of me illuminates the truth. When I would hear the adults around me say, "she's been here before", I no longer wonder why they would say that. Spiritual attunement is something every soul possesses, but unfortunately such spiritual acumen is snuffed out by needless indulgences and distractions.

We are the worst for such spiritual neglect. But you might beg to differ with all the myriads of religions and spiritual pursuits. When we no longer seek to attain divine connection by outward stimuli or for the sake of an experience, but rather by understanding our "is-ness", we will cease to suffer needlessly. "Normal" is the societal cultivation of an idea, philosophy, or creed. When any of us move outside of that construct, it's considered abnormal. When you decide to "BE", you will be considered "abnormal". I hope you'll be okay with that. The liberation of the "Self" is the most freeing and responsible thing one can do, which is honesty and truth from the depth of the soul.

The Killing of Self-Idolatry

Christ made His agreement to come to fulfill Purpose before he incarnated. The scriptures say He was crucified BEFORE the foundation of the world.

He knew His purpose, performed His function in the earth and then returned to the Eternal Spirit, having passed the tests and won the victory for the human experience, proving that this divine creature in all of its glory can even overcome death.

His life is our example of the human experience which requires The Faith, for The Function in order to Free the spirit from this body or grace of death to get the soul

back to its Ascended Higher Godlike Nature. WE have that same mandate. "As The Father has sent me, even so I send you." John 20:21 KJV

I cannot tell anyone how to grieve, how long to grieve or not to grieve. What I can do, in my part to serve humanity, is to give my human account as to having a *way* to grieve that produces health and the prosperity of spirit, soul and body.

I want the reader to know there is a healthy way to grieve and manage grief. It lies within you getting still and knowing yourself. It lies with you being as honest and truthful about how you feel and being willing to confront yourself.

What Now?

My entire life up until the point of my son's transition had prepared me for it. And as bitter as it is, I cannot deny the light of Truth within my soul.

If you are in grief's darkness and you don't know this light, I encourage you to find people that you can witness their light and begin to ask them for the hope that lies within them. The Most High God has not left you without a witness. I will encourage you to get as far away from the negative energies as you can. Start with the ones within yourself. Always look for the good and the positive in everything because it is a universal law, there's no positive without the negative.

Journal, meditate, pray and fast if you can, to put your mind in a submissive state. You will be amazed at how a simple walk can shift your mind's negative energy. This book is my honest expression of *my grief experience*. It's *my reality* of the days, years I spent in grief's grasp. I have several friends and many acquaintances who have traversed these treacherous waters before me, some healthily, some not so much. But whatever the case, a lesson awaits and I can only hope that it's learned, there is a healthy way to grieve.

My journey continues as I face each new moment with the understanding that we are all here for a limited number of moments and that each of them are meant to reveal to us an aspect of ourselves. As the seasons come and go, the cycles of life will continue. Imagine if a season got stuck and refused its natural order, oh how out of balance the ecosystem would be. So it goes for you dear reader, don't get stuck in any season no matter how beautiful or how sad..., it's only a season and this too shall pass. I don't say that flippantly, I say it with all sincerity. If you are in the initial stages of grief, be patient with yourself and those around you. Be determined and committed to your own healing.

Be intentional to activate from within the courage to face your pain and to accept what has happened. You cannot change it and no amount of rehearsing it or grieving it will alleviate the pain or fill the void. Above all, **live!** Take the memories of your loved one, the experience or the dream or whatever it is that you are grieving and use its energy to reproduce the love and the life it came to give. In this way, you are giving back to the world and the universe the needed light and love to heal all, beginning with yourself.

Thank you for making time for my read, as I've shared my story. I hope that you have found something useful to help you in your process. I love you and I say that with all sincerity. It's not because I know you, but it's because you are a human being and grief is an experience we all share.

Abundant Blessings,

Evelyn Rai

Follow me on social media, Facebook: @grief2grace or email me at Evelyn@EvelynRai.com or visit my website at www.EvelynRai.com

Credits & Acknowledgments

John Legend (Artist) - All Of Me: Written by John Legend, Toby Gad. Writer(s): John Legend, Toby Gad Love in the Future August 12, 2013.
Lyrics © Publishing Test Account, DistroKid, BMG Rights Management, Sony/ATV Music Publishing LLC

Dr. Caroline Leaf (Author) - "Who Switched Off My Brian". Published by Thomas Nelson, November 2009.

Winnie The Pooh, Eeyore, Tigger - Creator A. A. Milne: Illustrator E.H. Shepard. © Disney/Pixar. All Rights Reserved.

Florence Scovel Schinn (Author) - "The Game of Life and How to Play it". Published 1925.

Masaru Emoto (Author) - "The Hidden Messages in Water". Published September 20, 2005.

Dr. Joy Degruy (Author) - Post Trumatic Slave Symdrome Study : *America's Legacy of Enduring Injury and Healing* is a 2005 theoretical work by Joy DeGruy Leary. First published by Uptone Press in Milwaukie, Oregon in 2005, with a later re-release by the author in 2017.

Scripture References - King James, New American Standard and English Standard Versions

Etymology Website - https://www.etymonline.com/ © 2001-2022 Douglas Harper

About the Author

Music has the power to transport us to another time and place. Evelyn Rai harnesses that power through music and melodies that appeal to audiences of music lovers and fellow professionals alike. From a young age, She has found great joy and satisfaction in making music and sharing it with her dedicated fans.

As a Creative Director, Producer, Singer, and Songwriter, Evelyn Rai has many years of professional experience in various roles within the entertainment industry. With many singing and speaking credits to her accomplishment, Evelyn Rai says singing is her gift in service to humanity.

Life is filled with swift transitions. This author's first published work is written to share the heartfelt account of her experience with grief and the uncompromising power of God's relentless love and hope to meet a very human experience.

A professional speaker, teacher, performer and mother, Evelyn Rai will inspire you to embrace your humanity by understanding the greatness your *Divine Nature* within. She resides in Indianapolis, IN with her children and fur babies.

"How can someone traverse the waters of grief so unthinkable as the author's and become so richly generous in loving and caring for others? It seems an impossibility from my perspective. Nevertheless, the author continues to give even to the point of sharing her deepest pain so that others can ford the treacherous waters of grief. Besides the

book, I have witnessed the author's harrowing journey from grief to grace from close and afar. However, the author remains standing as a testimony to all of us who have suffered a loss. Therefore, I suggest reading her book and embracing the overflowing love and grace extended to you as you open your heart to its transforming thoughts, suggestions, and process. Those who embrace the outpouring of insight shared in her book will inspire to face each cycle of life with fresh hope, allow healing, and shake free from grief's grasp." - Dr. Cheryl A. Perkins; BS, MSM, Ph.D.

CPSIA information can be obtained
at www.ICGtesting.com
Printed in the USA
LVHW012211160523
747196LV00013B/364